Schindler's Gift

Schindler's Gift

How
One Man
Harnessed
ADHD
to
Change
the World

Kevin Roberts

Library of Congress Cataloguing-in-Publication Data
ISBN 978-0-9990155-1-3 (Paperback Edition)

Cover design by Cynthia Baldwin

Interior design and typesetting by Cynthia Baldwin

Photographs used by permission of The United State Holocaust Museum. The views or opinions expressed in this book, and the context in which the images are used, do not necessarily reflect the views or policy of, nor imply approval or endorsement by, the United States Holocaust Memorial Museum.

To Andrea Bilbow,
You demonstrate the extraordinary power of one loving mother
to change the world.

Contents

Foreword

The Oskar I Did Not Know: The ADHD Hero

By David Giwerc

This book is brilliantly conceived and superbly written about a hero who chose to risk his life for a purpose that ignited his heart. Even though his head should have told him there was great danger lurking with every human being he chose to save, he took risks to do the right thing. Kevin's book, the extensive research he conducted, the stories he tells of Schindler's bravery and the history of his life all form a mirror and accurate reflection of the painful struggles of many children and adults with undiagnosed ADHD. *Schindler's Gift* highlights the unique brain wiring that Oskar Schindler possessed, and shows the cerebral underpinnings that account for his shrewd, creative, and successful manipulation of the most ruthless and sociopathic regime in the history of mankind. Kevin also portrays the danger Oskar willingly exposed himself to because of his deep sense of compassion.

Kevin's book is personal to me because of the history of my family. There isn't a day that goes by where I don't think about the Holocaust and all six million Jews, including many of my relatives, who perished at the hands of the Nazis. My thoughts turn especially toward my great-grandfather, David Kneller, my namesake, who died in Auschwitz.

I gained pride, strength, and confidence; knowing the details of what my relatives went through, awareness that in my mind made every obstacle seem miniscule. I truly felt I could deal with any challenge, even learning how to deal with the seemingly invisible struggles of ADHD when I was first diagnosed as an adult. Most health care professionals in 1994, incidentally, said I could not have ADHD because I was an adult. I luckily found the right person to diagnose me and help me select the appropriate treatment. Any situation, task or challenge I had to face paled in comparison to what my parents and relatives experienced during the Holocaust.

It took many years before my dad was able to talk about his own tales of terror and the heinous acts of violence and killing he witnessed on a daily basis until his liberation. One particular story, chronicled in an amazing book, *Ordinary Men*, describes the events of the town my father lived in during his childhood and until his early teens, Jozefow. According to the book, "It was a typical Polish village of modest white houses with thatched roofs. Among its inhabitants were 1800 Jews." Eight of those Jews were my father, his two brothers, three sisters, and both parents.

On July 13, 1942 a police battalion was ordered by the Nazis to shoot and kill 1500 of the 1800 Jews in Jozefow. This battalion was ordered to round up the Jews. The book goes on to recount: "Male Jews of working age were to be separated and taken to a work camp." This most likely would have been the dreaded work-and-killing factory of Auschwitz. The book continues: "The remaining Jews—the women, and children, and elderly—were to be shot on the spot by the battalion." Of the 1800 Jews of that small village in central Poland, 300 survived. On that same darkest of days, a miracle of light also occurred. My father and his entire family survived extermination.

I strongly believe it was my father's ADHD that allowed him to survive WWII and the Holocaust. Like many with ADHD, my father was a natural rebel, an instinctual risk-taker, one who thrived under intensity. I believe ADHD also played a major role in his success, coming to the United States with only an eighth-grade education and becoming one of the most successful builders in the capital district of upstate NY.

Many of the traits that Oskar Schindler employed in his brilliant, shrewd manipulation of the Nazi regime—which ultimately saved 1200 Jewish families—were traits my father exhibited to survive the Holocaust, to endure beyond the utter destruction of his hometown while witnessing the slaughter of 1500 of his fellow Jews.

Oskar Schindler witnessed such events, and having been friends with Jewish people since he was a small boy, he eventually felt he had to do something about it. Oskar Schindler was able to manipulate with strategic intention and hyper-focus, and he used these abilities to save families from the deadly actions of the Nazis. My father also had these traits, especially a hyper-focus of intense energy with a clear intention of his daily and long-term mission. Without an extraordinary sense of mission, people like Oskar and my father often struggle in life.

Of course, the apple does not fall too far from the tree, so the same hyper-focus my dad possessed also became part of my new modus operandi when I was diagnosed with ADHD at age thirty-eight. Learning about my dad, and now Oskar Schindler, has helped to reinforce my understanding of ADHD and the paradoxical challenges and strengths it can manifest in one's life. We can all learn how to manage both the challenges and successes that often accompany ADHD. Following a powerful sense of mission, I decided to become an ADHD Coach, and in 1998 to create what would eventually become the first and most comprehensive accredited ADHD Coaching training program in the world. I wanted to help every person with ADHD understand that they had gifts to give to the world.

This brings me to another important message that Kevin so articulately and convincingly conveys. It is about the pervasive focus on the negative messages kids receive from a young age into adulthood, especially when they don't perform based on the established standards prescribed by society. Oskar Schindler did not follow the rules and did not do well in school. For his entire life, he did things *his* way, with numerous negative repercussions. However, when human lives depended on his actions, he was roused to persist, focus and stay motivated. Twelve-hundred Jewish families survived as a result, and the descendants and successive generations of their families have lived on, leading productive and fulfilling lives thanks to the unique brain wiring and passion-driven personality of Oskar Schindler.

In spite of Schindler's example, the bulk of published research and education on adult ADHD has extensively documented the impairments and struggles with the disorder. This prevailing focus has helped to increase the awareness of the challenges experienced by adults with ADHD, and has also highlighted the importance of obtaining proper diagnosis and treatment with a well-trained ADHD healthcare professional. Schindler did not have access to ADHD medications, but now we have numerous medications, along with behavioral interventions, that help modern-day *Schindlers* achieve a consistent sense of purpose and success in their lives.

Kevin identifies a number of positive, life-changing attributes which Oskar Schindler demonstrated daily despite the many business failings he had experienced, which were most likely due to his undiagnosed, untreated ADHD and his lack of knowledge about his own strengths and weaknesses. However, despite all the challenges he faced, he saved human lives by accessing his strengths—passion, a delight in intensity, and hyper-focus—to take the greatest action one person can do for others: he chose to save the lives of his fellow human beings in Krakow, Poland, regardless of religion, race, or ethnicity.

When you read this book you will have a different perception about the potential often wired into ADHD people. I learned about the depth of love one man can have for a people, a race of human beings that the Nazis and most of Europe was dedicated to annihilating. But I also discovered that this horrible period gave Oskar some elements that all people with ADHD need to thrive: intensity, support, and a sense of intention-driven purpose. Oskar's failure before and after the war, and his glorious success during that horrific period, serve as a beacon to how people with ADHD can change themselves and transform the world.

I thank Kevin from the deepest place in my heart for writing this amazing book about a special man who exemplifies the very best in humanity and for presenting the world with a new ADHD hero. This book should be read by everyone challenged by ADHD and the people who support them. I have been an ADHD coach for over twenty years. I know what people with ADHD can create in their lives when their attention is aligned with their intention. Like Oskar Schindler, they also can create a lasting, purposeful masterpiece. I have seen people with ADHD who understood it, and who understood how their divine character strengths and capacities could be used to positively transform the world. My hope is that you will use this book to help yourself and help others change the world.

David Giwerc
Founder, ADD Coach Academy
Author of *Permission to Proceed*

Acknowledgments

- Robin O'Neil, for the passion to research Schindler's life. Your passion ignited a fire in me.
- David Crowe, for painstaking research that gave me the raw material to make my case. Also, for graciously talking with me by phone and confirming many of my suspicions.
- Steven Spielberg, I have never talked to you, but *Schindler's List* changed my life and the lives of many young people I have worked with. Your film gave me the impetus to research Schindler's life because you gave me the unmistakable suspicion that Oskar had ADHD. Without you, this book, and several trips I have led for ADHD teenagers to Poland would not have happened. The mention of your name evokes a deep sense of gratitude in me. Thank you!
- Dr. Erica Rosenberg, for your work on Emilie's biography, your willingness to help me and your passion for telling the Schindler saga to the world.
- Joseph Biederman, for being willing to make room in your busy schedule to meet with me, and discuss the fact that Schindler saved your parents. You Rock, Doc!
- Ben Kassab, for clearly showing me what Oskar Schindler must have been like as a young man.
- The Casman family, for mentoring me on my path of Jew in Training (JIT).

- The Block family, for completing the training that the Casman family started.

- Rabbi Aaron Goldstein, for showing me many years ago that Judaism is mostly about love and compassion.

- Phil Parker, for helping me with this manuscript, offering me great insight, which was all incorporated into this book.

- Andrew Johnson, for helping me in the editing process and offering me great insight into the flow of this book.

- Cindy Dean Baldwin, for injecting your life and passion into this design. The cover still gives me shivers! You nailed my vision so perfectly.

- Rob and Saskia Pereira, for introducing my vision of Schindler to the Netherlands and for being the parents I always wish I had had.

- Barbaji, for showing me that some people change the world with one small act of kindness at a time.

- Liz Borino, for believing in me and caring enough to give me great feedback.

- Terri Schell, for embracing and adding to my vision, and helping the final form of the book coalesce into a unified whole.

- Kelly Campion, for showing me that some of the most powerful people are the ones who work quietly behind the scenes.

- Tony Bilbow, for your excellent feedback and insight, and your affirmation of my TV-viewing choices.

- Chris Sarver, for pushing me to organize my first trip to Poland, Auschwitz and Schindler's factory with ADHD teens. That life-changing adventure would not have happened without your loving challenge and encouragement.

- David Giwerc, for writing the foreword and for deeply affirming my humanity.

- Christopher Caretti, for your deep compassion and humanity that continues to be a source of inspiration to me. You have a lot of Schindler in you!

- Colin McGee, for your constant support of me and this book. You gave me great feedback, much of which was incorporated. You also helped me with my post-house-fire PTSD.

- Doug Rutley, for being one of the only people with whom I can watch Holocaust documentaries. You should know that you are far more intelligent and talented than you give yourself credit for. Thank you, also, for being my NWC (Night Watchman Coordinator). Charnwood.

- Peggy Belan, for the wisdom of nahr hing.

- Steve and Peggy Kassab, for giving me a great example of how to love and support a child who is clearly a Schindler.

- Tim Kowalski, for teaching me that all people are worth saving, a lesson Oskar Schindler's example helped to reinforce.

- Joe Bilbow, for boldly demonstrating that change is possible.

- Jane Stewart, for giving me honest and powerful feedback, which led to my making this book more engaging and extraordinarily more interesting.

- Patty Payette, Ms. P., for being a wonderful human being and ongoing cheerleader who sees my gifts better than I do.

- Emily and Sagar, for bringing joy to my life by showing me the power of love.

- Dan Campion, for showing me that impulsive people, like Oskar Schindler, often have huge hearts. When I needed a drainage ditch, you showed up. When my roof leaked, you rushed over. When someone you do not know has a flat tire, you pull off to help. You also take great risks to help other people, putting yourself in danger. You have a lot in common with Oskar Schindler.

- Marko Ferek and Jerry Mills, for being my traveling buddies and showing me how ADHD people are often superhuman when on an adventure.

- The Bargwich, for showing us that just because something reliably evokes a certain image does not prevent us from adding in our own creative spin, something that Oskar Schindler would certainly have appreciated.

- Alex Sapick, for being a powerful example of persistence and humility.

- Joey Dery, for showing me so much of myself, and for never giving up.

- Miss Missie, Noah, and John Stein, for being wonderful kindred spirits who make me feel that I am OK. You guys help keep me inspired. Zellstein.

- Thelma, for showing me and the world that sometimes "jinkies" is really the right thing to say.

- Yuuh, Lars, and Kod, for filling my day with innocent, albeit repetitive, fun. Fun is the currency that helps me finish writing a book! I need all three of you.

- Amy Campbell, for being one of my most powerfully loving allies in my time of need.

- Kath, for putting weight on me, and helping bring me back to life.

- Patrick Campion, for showing me that a gruff exterior is often accompanied by an incredibly loving heart.

Introduction

The story of Oskar Schindler has been told on screen, in books and articles, and appears all over the Internet. I owe a great debt in this book to Steven Spielberg, Dr. Ball-Kaduri, Robin O'Neil, Thomas Keneally, David Crowe, Mietek Pemper, and Emilie Schindler. Without their research and hard work I could never have completed this book. I do not seek to retell Schindler's tale, so much as to offer a more nuanced appreciation for the totality of who he was and why his life turned out the way it did. He was not a typical man in any way, a fact that has both positive and negative implications. By discovering his inner workings, we can move toward an understanding of what allowed him to become a supreme altruist as well as a total failure. We do ourselves a great service by giving equal consideration to both sides. Schindler offers us a kernel of hope of the magnanimous possibility that exists within us all, but also provides us a warning about the potential pitfalls along the path. Oskar Schindler is a beacon for the transformative potential wired into each and every human being.

Uninformed individuals frequently suggest ADHD is not real. Despite a huge body of scientific evidence, many still maintain that ADHD results from poor character, laziness, and bad parenting. While ample evidence exists to show that numerous gene variants correlate with ADHD, these detractors are not swayed, primarily because they do not have any interest in objectively observing the data. Science does not seem to factor into their opinion. Another group of uninformed people vociferously maintains that the Holocaust did not happen. Some nation states have even sponsored Holocaust-denial conferences. In many countries around the world, Holocaust-denying books are among the top sellers. A recent book released by a medical doctor also denied the existence of ADHD, sparking such interest that hundreds of thousands of copies have been sold. With deniers of both ADHD and the Holocaust, junk science, prejudice, and ignorance prevail. Thousands of studies make a clear and compelling case for ADHD being a condition that derives from differences in the brain, the neurobiological environment of an individual and genetic makeup. Likewise, the existence of the horrors of the Holocaust not only rests on the testimony of tens of thousands of eyewitnesses, but also on hundreds of millions, yes you read that number correctly, hundreds of millions of documents. Examining both of these topics, this book endeavors to ground its assertions in science and the historical record.

My journey into both of these topics intensified after watching an Academy-Award-winning movie, Steven Spielberg's epic, *Schindler's List*. I own several copies of the DVD and have watched it at least fifty times. It serves as an old, reliable source of inspiration. With some movies, one talks and thinks about them, but *Schindler's List* arouses my humanity, fueling an impulse to do something to help the human race. The message of redemption of the movie entrances me. A man who drank too much, gambled, philandered, and joined the Nazi party, single-handedly saved more Jews than any other person during the Holocaust. Honored by Israel as one of the "Righteous among the Nations," he risked his own life time and again, and spent his entire fortune to save lives. Yitzhak Stern, who owed his life to Schindler, said it this way: "Brothers, in the Hebrew language there are three terms, three grades: person, man, human being. I believe there is a fourth one: 'Schindler.'"

I met a man in Spielberg's movie who I wanted to be more like. I resonated with Oskar Schindler in a way that made me want to live with some of the same courage, creativity, and tireless service that he offered humanity during those few years in Kraków. His impact on me has been so profound that I learned Polish so that I could visit Kraków and Schindler's factory. I have taken families and young people with ADHD to Poland, Auschwitz, and Schindler's factory, and have watched Schindler's example transform lives right in front of me. I wanted to get inside the man's head and figure out how and why he was able to work so much magic in the midst of the Holocaust.

Before and after the war, I learned, Schindler did not have an easy life, struggling with his marriage and serially unsuccessful in business, not to mention, significant academic problems during his school years and numerous brushes with the law. The disparity between the great difficulties that plagued him throughout life and the genius that emerged during the war sent me into reflection. How could a man so supremely capable of navigating the corrupt, if not psychopathic, network of Nazi bureaucracy fail so utterly in almost every other endeavor?

Delving in to the details, a portrait that was very familiar to me emerged. Oskar had had a troubled home life, did not do well in school, and was a hands-on and kinesthetic learner. He teemed with creativity, but easily tired of routines and the mundane details of running a business. He seemed to thrive on taking unnecessary risks and was drawn to recklessly adventurous pursuits, some that put his very life in peril. Restlessness plagued him, so much so that he abandoned his wife on many occasions to follow some fleeting passion, or new woman, of the moment. He struggled to control his impulses, and was even arrested for assault on several occasions. Addiction ran in his family. He and his father both suffered from alcoholism, and Oskar had some gambling issues as well. For most of Oskar's life, he was a mess.

In the cauldron of World War II and the Holocaust, many of his liabilities and shortcomings became strengths, and the intensity and severity of the situation allowed an abject failure to access his true inner genius. I have seen this dichotomy many times before, which is perhaps why Oskar Schindler seemed so familiar to me, like someone I had known my whole life.

I have ADHD; I have worked for almost two decades with ADHD people; I have written articles and books on ADHD, as well having a Master's degree in ADHD Studies. While such a condition was not medically diagnosed for most of his life, Oskar Schindler was clearly an ADHD individual. He exhibited many of the strengths and weaknesses inherent in the condition, a fact that convincingly helps account for both his successes and failures. This book lays out a well-documented case to back up these assertions, and rests soundly on the belief that Oskar was a gifted man who was able to access that giftedness because of the crises of the times and the support of a few key Jewish partners. More importantly, Schindler was, at heart, a good man, a fact often obscured by his penchant for deviance and life on the edge. While the great achievement of his life rests on saving 1,200 people, the greatest tragedy can be found in his inability to save himself. Without the intensity of the war years, and the daily support from extremely talented individuals, Oskar did not cope well.

The message of his life, therefore, is twofold. First, his example shows the potential for redemption, that the core of the human heart has the capacity to stand up to evil. Secondly,

Schindler shows us that, without treatment, ADHD and addiction can ruin our lives. I often wonder what other tremendous feats he could have pulled off had Oskar Schindler been able to find the appropriate support and intensity that would have allowed his genius to continue to flourish.

As you read this book, please realize that I am inviting you to learn lessons to help yourself and others. The most overlooked lesson of Schindler's life is that he was able to do extraordinary things when he had extraordinary support. After the war, his Jewish workers and partners did help him financially, but Oskar tried to go it alone, following his fancy into one ill-advised business scheme after another. With support, Oskar was a towering genius; without it, he was a miserable wretch, prone to extreme mood swings of anger and depression. Without ADHD, he would not have been such a failure after the war, but he would not have been able, as well, to do what he did during the war.

Whether you have ADHD or are simply one of those people who has not accomplished what you are capable of, read this book as a manual to help yourself so that you can fulfill your dreams, and help other people fulfill theirs. You will receive in these pages an essential primer to the Holocaust. You will come away with a broad understanding of the life of Oskar Schindler. You will see that this man had ADHD, and you will understand this condition in a way that will allow you to identify both its positives and negatives.

I maintain that a large percentage of the people who change this world for the better probably have ADHD. I hope that when you finish this book, you will have a road map to change yourself and the world.

—*Kevin Roberts*

Chapter 1 The Oskars of the World

If a man does not keep pace with his companions, perhaps it is because he hears a different drummer. Let him step to the music which he hears, however measured or far away.

—Henry David Thoreau

The Red Army Approaches

IN THE WEE HOURS of May 9, 1945, the Red Army rumbled toward Oskar Schindler's factory in Czechoslovakia. Instant death awaited Oskar, a Nazi Party member and war profiteer, if he was captured by the Soviets. Twelve hundred Jewish workers were determined to not let that happen. Led by Yitzhak Stern and Mietek Pemper, they scrambled and hurriedly composed letters of safe conduct for Oskar and his wife. They went so far as to write these letters in Hebrew, English, and Russian. They detailed the many unbelievable feats Oskar had pulled off to save them, risking his own life over and over again. The leaders of this band of Jewish survivors were intimately acquainted with Schindler's heroic deeds, and they wrote about Oskar pulling Jews off of Auschwitz-bound trains, saving whole families from execution, and spending his entire fortune to bribe Nazi officials so that his workers would live to tell their story:

1

"Twelve hundred of us are alive only because of the selfless heroism of Oskar Schindler. Please do whatever you can to help this man."

Simon Jeret, one of Oskar's Jewish workers, gave his gold fillings so that Oskar could be sent off with a token of their esteem and gratitude. The gold was quickly melted down and forged into a ring, on the inside of which was written a line from a sacred text of Judaism, the Talmud: "Whoever saves one life saves the world entire." The twelve hundred workers assembled on the factory floor as Oskar Schindler and his wife were about to make their escape and attempt to flee to the American lines. A dozen or so of his workers came forward and presented him with the letters and the gold ring. Oskar handed the letters to his wife, Emilie, who stood by his side, and held up the ring, which glistened as the factory flood lights shone from above. As he stood there and gazed at what may well have been the most precious gift he had ever received, the previous six years flashed through his mind in an instant.

"Why on earth are you moving to Kraków?" Emilie had asked him at the end of September 1939. "For the first time in your life, you're making a good living. We're saving money, living well. Why do you want to throw that all away?"[1]

"I'm not throwing it away, Emilie," Oskar replied. "I'm adding to it. I am going to make us wealthy beyond our wildest dreams."[2]

"But why Kraków? Can't you stay here in Czechoslovakia and do the same thing?"

"Kraków is where things are happening. That is where the money is to be made."[3]

He waved his hand and stared out the window, as if his mind was already in Kraków. Emilie knew there was no stopping him. She had been through several of Oskar's get-rich-quick schemes. His words offered no comfort, but rather sent

Schindler with his office employees at Emalia, 1940. *United States Holocaust Memorial Museum, courtesy of Leopold Page Photographic Collection*

her into a disquieted acceptance of a reality she knew she could not change. She was certain that Oskar would rack up yet another failure.

But now, six years later, she looked up at the glistening gold ring, and realized she had been terribly wrong. Oskar *had* achieved wealth beyond their wildest dreams; twelve hundred people stood in front of her, testifying to that fact. Oskar could not take his eyes off the ring. He stared at it, savoring the moment, even as the din of Russian artillery in the distance disrupted the calm sanctity of the moment.

Success had always eluded him. From a doomed chicken farming operation to a failed bid as a tractor salesman, Oskar could never manage to follow through on details. Even with his meteoric rise on the motorcycle racing circuit, he struggled to persist. In less than a year, he had gone from an amateur to a professional motorcycle racer, won some big races, and then quit without explanation. Oskar seemed to have an innate impulse to sabotage his chances for success. In 1938, he was actually hired by the German army for a job he seemed well suited for: sabotage and espionage. He was arrested by the Czechoslovak authorities less than three weeks into this endeavor and almost paid with his life.

But here he was now in front of these people who owed him their very lives. He knew in every minute millimeter of his being that he was finally a success. The gold ring stood as a symbol of the gold inside of Oskar. Like precious ore trapped in a deep, subterranean mine, Oskar was never able to tap into that gold. The Holocaust changed all that, giving him the psychological dynamite that blasted a hole in his being and, in turn, caused his gold to come forth, allowing the genius of Oskar Schindler to finally emerge. He set up a factory to make money, but then brilliantly used this operation as a safe haven to keep Jewish workers safe from Nazi murderers. With the end of the war and the atrocities of the Nazis, however, that hole closed up again, and Oskar, like someone who had temporarily awoken from a coma, went back into a long slumber of depression, addiction, and abject failure. How could a man beset with so many inner demons and outer flaws end up defeating one of the most barbaric and evil mindsets the world has ever known? And why was his success so short lived?

Troubled Youth

Oskar's upbringing was a proving ground. "You never finish anything,"[4] Oskar's father told him at least once a day. The elder Schindler had many of the same troublesome tendencies he loathed in his son, but did not know how to help him. Both possessed a high level of intelligence, but the Schindlers were underachievers. His father had a business, but it never succeeded the way the elder Schindler had hoped. Father and son struggled to fully and effectively use their gifts, as well as to simply get along with one another on a day-to-day basis. The Schindler household teemed with arguments, frequent fights, and constant belittling. Oskar was born into a conflict-ridden home, a situation that followed him into school and life.

Troubled youth like Oskar pass through my door every working day. They are my livelihood. I am essentially an academic coach who specializes in Attention Deficit Hyperactivity Disorder (ADHD) and underachievers of many stripes. The young people I serve hate school, like Oskar Schindler certainly did, and by the time they make their way to me, they have received a steady diet of denigration. School forces people like Oskar to perform against their grain. They are often hands-on learners, mechanically gifted, high energy, and exceptionally social. School requires them to sit still and contain their energy, creativity, and their desire to "do something." School, by way of tests and reports cards, does not measure their true gifts, the ones they will likely employ as adults. They are evaluated on a narrow band of aptitudes, and taught in a way that pathologizes their neurological hard-wiring. Their way of being is simply wrong in the view of most of their teachers, and maybe even their parents. This message will not be delivered in a memo, but will be reinforced over and over again by snide remarks, under-the-breath insults, dirty looks, and sometimes overt declarations. Like Oskar Schindler as a young man, they will hear, both explicitly and implicitly, variations of these worn-out lines, which take on a life of their own, comprising negative internal dialogue that will never completely go away:

- You're lazy.
- You're not good enough.
- You're flawed.
- There's something wrong with you.
- You'll never amount to anything.
- You're trouble, and I don't have the time or energy for someone like you.

- I find you irritating.
- You make me sick.
- You're not worth it.
- You never do anything right.
- You always make mistakes.
- You *are* a mistake.

These types of negative messages usually belie incredible, and often untapped, talents. These external voices become internalized, and a sense of toxic shame, a feeling of being irreparably flawed, roots itself deep in the psyche. They try, and try, and try to *change*. Eventually, faced with the onslaught of repeated academic failure, they give up, and believe that they're just not up to the challenge. I have seen this happen as early as second grade, and sometimes these young people make it all the way to college before they finally give up.

They lose faith in their ability to cope, and see themselves as broken, even though they may not admit this in casual conversation. By early adolescence, many of them start gravitating toward others who have also taken on such toxic messages about themselves. These associations of marginalized young people easily evolve into deviance. They start smoking cigarettes, maybe marijuana, spraying graffiti, engaging in petty vandalism, and simply trying to find some passion in their lives, or at least negative intensity. Their early experiences often lead them to attempt to find adventure, intensity, and excitement in unproductive and self-sabotaging ways, and brushes with the law can ensue.

By the time they come to me, a lot of psychological damage has been done, and while I am ostensibly here to help them succeed in school, the first order of business is to begin counteracting the many destructive messages they have absorbed. I have found no better way of achieving this purpose than by

Hollywood Portrayal

Schindler's List, Spielberg's masterpiece, is faithful to the essential details of Oskar Schindler and his life. However, as might be expected from a Hollywood production, cinematic necessities led to a few minor changes. For example, Yitzhak Stern is portrayed as Schindler's plant manager, accountant, and contact in Płaszów Camp, and he is involved in his black market activities. In reality, three men assisted Schindler in his commercial and humanitarian endeavors: Yitzhak Stern, Mietek Pemper, and Abraham Bankier. In addition, Oskar's time as a spy for the German army is not covered at all by Spielberg, which is significant because the contacts he made from these activities are key to understanding his success in saving his Jewish workers. Nevertheless, those who lived the story and who knew Schindler well believe the movie captures the essence of the man and his extraordinary experience. It is a movie that changes lives, and it put me on my present path of helping people with ADHD. Mr. Spielberg, you are a man who changed my life and the light you shed on Schindler is changing other people's lives as well. Thank you!

filling their heads with stories of successful ADHDers. They need to know that people just like them have gone on to do extraordinary things. In addition to stories, I have at my disposal many successful ADHDers in the community who are willing to come and talk to my students. I know an ADHD man who puts out oil fires, another who has a demolition business, and even an ADHD dentist who got into dental school without having a college degree. Their personal tales are filled with getting in trouble, adventurous missteps, and ultimately succeeding in life by their own, often unorthodox, methods. These young people hear such stories and start to hope, for the first time in perhaps several years.

No ADHD individual has inspired them and given them more hope than Oskar Schindler. I talk all the time about Oskar and relate details of his life to theirs. "You're another Schindler," I will often say. "Are you going to help people like he did or are you going to add to their suffering?" I own several copies of the movie *Schindler's List*, the award-winning 1993 movie directed by Steven Spielberg that dramatized Oskar's story, and I regularly insist that my students and clients watch it. Many challenge my assertion that he had ADHD. I then share my research about his life. When I get into the details with them, though, they quickly change their minds.

School Hater

Like any good ADHD individual, Oskar Schindler hated school. It seems to have been a breeding ground for lying, cheating, and deception. Many ADHD people become excellent liars because we so frequently experience finger-pointing, fault-finding, and exasperation focused in our direction. Born in 1908, Schindler went to grade school, Volksschule, in his hometown of Svitavy, a city that for the first ten years of his life was part of the Austro-Hungarian Empire. For a short time, Oskar attended Realschule, similar to high school, before enrolling at the Höheres Realgymnasium, a technical school similar to a vocational or trade school today.[5] This type of institution was meant to produce mining, mechanical, and civil engineers, as well as other practical-based trades that would fill the needs of the industrial installations in that region.[6] Oskar's enrollment at this technical school is the first sign in the historical record that he was not academically oriented, a fact which he reiterated frequently: "I'm a businessman, not a

8

scholar."[7] He failed and was forced to repeat grade nine. Two years later, in 1924, Oskar was expelled for "forging his grade report."[8] His reputation for cheating in school and a tendency toward petty crime earned him an unflattering nickname. Children in Svitavy would often yell at the sight of Oskar, "Hey, look! It's Schindler the swindler."[9]

The lack of a feeling of competence in school is a major factor that pushes people like Oskar toward deviant behaviors.[10] Oskar's energies were not trained on conforming to the system, but rather on using his powers of deception and manipulation to try to defeat it. Without this inclination, over a thousand more victims would have perished at the hands of the Nazis, and many more thousands would never have been born. As you will see, one of Oskar's qualities was to turn negatives into powerful positives.

From all available data and reports, Oskar was a tactile and kinesthetic learner, one who learned in a hands-on way and required movement along with physical purpose to drive his actions and intentions. From a very young age, Oskar gravitated toward anything mechanical. Around town, he was often spotted with a spanner, a tool to undo nuts and bolts, and an oily rag or two hanging out of one of his pockets.[11] He loved taking apart machines and putting them back together again, and delighted in fixing things.

Such children have often been considered difficult to teach, and they can become the object of scorn. Even today, many adolescents considered at-risk tend to be highly tactual, needing hands-on learning experiences, and kinesthetic learners, needing frequent movement.[12] Traditional learning environments just do not meet their needs. Oskar Schindler certainly would be considered at-risk in today's educational systems. He would be referred for therapy, coaching, and with some of his acting out might even be forced to go to an "alternative" school for those who fail to succeed in the traditional academic environment. Just like the highly successful Jewish businessmen who helped and supported Oskar during the war, some of his teachers would have recognized Oskar's gifts and reminded him how smart he was, but the majority would have expressed consternation at his unwillingness to try harder. Like many ADHDers, he would ultimately have been called lazy and oppositional.

Oskar lived in an area known as the Sudetenland that was populated largely by people of German ethnicity. When he was born, that region was controlled by the Austro-Hungarian Empire; Oskar's family actually traced its history to the city of Vienna in Austria, which is something that would help him later on when he met Amon Göth, the Vienna-born Nazi brute whom he masterfully outwitted in his effort to save his Jewish workers. Although not born in Germany, Oskar identified as distinctly German. He spoke Polish and Czech and knew some Yiddish, but German was his mother tongue. According to witnesses, he spoke that language in an eloquent manner, one of many traits that endeared him to the Nazis.

After World War I, the Sudeten area, so named because of the Sudeten Mountains, became part of a brand new nation, Czechoslovakia, because the Austro-Hungarian Empire, one of World War I's losers, was split apart. Oskar was still educated according to the German system, and his instructors actually spoke German in the classroom. The part of Czechoslovakia Oskar lived in was also administered largely by Austrians and Germans. The Language Law of 1920 permitted minorities, like the Sudeten Germans, to receive school instruction in their own languages. The German-speaking people of Czechoslovakia, however, went from a position of dominance under the Austro-Hungarian Empire to that of minority, a fact that led to serious conflicts in the new nation,[13] conflicts that Adolf Hitler would eventually exploit in his bid to conquer Europe. Oskar grew up feeling like he was part of an underprivileged and battered minority, a fact that explains his support of the Nazi rise to power.

The German educational principles that operated in the schools Oskar attended had been set forth in Germany and Austria in the nineteenth century.[14] This system sought to foster certain values in the students and make them useful to the state.[15] It was a system designed to create:

1. Obedient soldiers for the army.

2. Obedient workers in the mines.

3. Well-subordinated civil servants for the government.

4. Well-subordinated clerks for industry.

5. Citizens who thought alike about major issues.[16]

This system of enforced conformity, obedience, and rote memorization made Oskar Schindler bristle. Oskar was anything but obedient, and perhaps could even be considered a natural rebel. At least nowadays we have Individual Education Programs (IEPs) and the law mandates accommodation for people with ADHD and other learning challenges. In Oskar's time, he and others like him were just seen as mutants whose defiance needed to be stamped out. Parenting and teaching approaches in Oskar's homeland were directed toward breaking the will of the child in order to produce an obedient subject, with the aid of force, manipulation, and repression.[17] It was very common for German school boys, and boys in many countries at that time, to be punished in front of the class with a strap that was designed for this purpose. The teacher would sit facing the class and would take a boy over his knee, whipping him until the boy began to cry. In some cases, such punishment did break a child's will. But in Oskar's case, it only made him more determined and defiant. Incidentally, Oskar went against the grain in many areas, not just school. He did not share in the rampant anti-Semitism that was common among Germans and other groups at that time. He developed many close friendships with Jewish children, a fact that he insisted played a role in his wartime heroism.

Rebels do not usually do well in any school, let alone the rigid Germanic educational institutions of the early twentieth century. Oskar was such a poor student that he did not even take the admissions exam to get into a university. Instead, he went to several trade schools and studied heaters, machinery, and chauffeuring, receiving certifications in all three of these areas.[18] Oskar Schindler was a doer. He had little patience for theories unless he could see some practical application. When he saw a way to apply knowledge, he was in his element.

The normal and mundane rhythms of academic life are not usually sufficient to arouse the ADHD brain. Danger, discomfort, and intensity, however, can really get our ADHD brains going. Many of us require extreme forms of stimulation to allow us to perform tasks and concentrate. The silver lining is that we often blossom under pressure. Thom Hartmann has talked much about the hunter archetype as a way of viewing ADHD. According to Hartmann's persuasive thesis, hunters are those individuals who respond quickly, sometimes instantaneously, to new stimuli. They thrive on the excitement of the chase and can switch gears at a moment's notice. These are exactly the same attributes that get ADHD kids in trouble when we put them into the classroom and expect them to sit in a desk all day, while bombarding them with information that interests them very little. Ah, but add an element of danger and excitement, and the ADHD brain begins to activate. The intensity of World War II helps account for Oskar being able to find his stride.[19] Generals George S. Patton and Ulysses S. Grant also shared this way of being; both men performed poorly in academic settings. These two military geniuses, like Oskar Schindler, changed the course of history. Schindler, Patton, and Grant all struggled with excessive drinking, mood issues, and malaise when not fully engaged in a grand pursuit. Patton, in addition, is widely believed to have suffered from another liability ADHDers are often diagnosed with: dyslexia. He, too, loved tinkering with mechanical objects and single-handedly developed America's first tank attack.

The Fast Lane

Given Oskar's mechanically-oriented nature, penchant for adventure, and hunger for excitement, his fascination with fast cars and motorcycles is easy to fathom. Oskar's father encouraged his son's interest in this area. Several family photos exist with Oskar driving while clad in a helmet and goggles. He liked to drive fast! Were he a teen today, he would have a fast car with a loud muffler, replete with custom modifications, and armed with thunderous subwoofers.

Like many ADHD young men today who have an innate aptitude for intense sports—bungee jumping, skateboarding, and snowboarding, for example—Oskar exhibited a natural ability with motorcycles.[20] He was known as the "speed demon" with the red Galloni 500 motorcycle, which also had a side car.[21] Even more interesting, this was supposedly the only motorcycle of its kind in Czechoslovakia.[22] Oskar liked attention, and he definitely operated under the mindset, "if you've got it, flaunt it."

Soon after getting his first motorcycle at age seventeen, Oskar started competing in races, and exhibited an ongoing and escalating need for speed. In 1928, he bought a 250 cm Königsswellen Moto-Guzzi, which at that time was supposed to be one of the fastest motorcycles in Europe.[23] A detailed account of a few of Oskar's races was given by his childhood friend, Ernst Tragatsch. His first official course started in the

Schindler and his father, Hans, with Schindler's roadster outside their home in Svitavy, 1929. *United States Holocaust Memorial Museum, courtesy of Leopold Page Photographic Collection*

city of Brno in Czechoslovakia and wound through the mountainous countryside:

> Oskar, riding his red Moto-Guzzi, finished third in his first race. His third-place victory so thrilled Oskar that he soon entered another race on the Alvater course, on the German border. Oskar competed with nine other racers in his motorcycle class. This time, though, two other racers also drove Moto-Guzzis. During most of the race, Oskar remained in fifth place. He moved into fourth place when one of his competitors on a Moto-Guzzi dropped out. He took third place when Kurt Henkelmann, a seasoned rider on a Werks-DKW, ran out of gas. As Henkelmann pushed his motorcycle towards the finish line, Oskar passed him, thinking he was in third place. For some unknown reason, Oskar

stopped just before the finish line, much to the dismay of the crowd, which shouted for him to cross over it. While he was mistaking their shouts for applause, Henkelmann pushed his motorcycle over the finish line to take third place.[24]

"Stopped just before the finish line" is a phrase that easily describes a good amount of ADHD behavior. Oskar did cross the finish line often enough, though, to be featured in the magazine, *Sport*, that same year, but for some reason, he did not continue motorcycle racing. It has amazed me over the years how ADHD people enjoy great initial success, but stop short of total mastery of whichever activities they happen to be pursuing. This tendency can be understood by appreciating the ADHD brain, which is constructed in such a way that it works well when something is new and exciting, but struggles to stay active when that same activity or interest becomes old hat, routine.

Like many ADHD people, Oskar Schindler demonstrated incredible talent that was never fully actualized because of lack of follow-through. Still, Oskar's racing expertise offers a great window into his character. Thriving in the intensity of physical exhilaration and danger, along with the very real possibility of injury and death, takes a rare set of physical and mental attributes that few possess.

Daredevil Geniuses

Well-known sports psychologist Dr. Deborah Graham did a statistical analysis on successful racing competitors and made a number of important findings that help us more fully appreciate Oskar Schindler. Coupled with a need to take risks, a quality common in ADHD-ers, Oskar possessed the skills required to be a successful race car driver.

Dominance: This crucial trait leads to being assertive and competitive, qualities which Oskar would show time and again in his dealings with the Nazis. He was an alpha male who did not shy away from conflict, a crucial attribute for someone who locked horns with one of history's most brutal and sadistic regimes.

Shrewdness: Dr. Graham's findings suggest that "a champion maintains a keen balance between being unpretentious and genuine, and being socially aware, diplomatic and calculating."[25] Obviously, to successfully save almost twelve hundred Jews from mass murderers bent on their extermination required incredible shrewdness. Oskar built friendships with the right people and called in favors at the right time. One misstep and the Holocaust would have claimed twelve hundred more victims.

Relaxation: This is the ability to keep composure in sometimes horrifically intense situations, which was a skill Oskar displayed time and again. He regularly intervened to rescue friends and workers from the clutches of the Nazis. Those around him remarked at his coolness and relaxation under pressure. Steven Spielberg's film depicts this quality when Schindler rescues Stern from the extermination-camp-bound train. When dealing with uncooperative Nazis in this scene, he says: "Gentlemen, thank you very much. I think I can guarantee you you'll both be in Southern Russia before the end of the month. Good day."[26] The two men gave in to the cool-as-a-cucumber Schindler and helped him pull Stern off the train. Grace under pressure often inspires fear in others!

Intelligence: The champion drivers Dr. Graham tested were consistently above average in abstract thinking, and they exhibited high levels of adaptability, flexibility, and the capacity to use concepts and generalizations to solve problems by drawing logical conclusions from a set of observations. Oskar demonstrated a mastery of abstract and adaptive thinking consistently. Whenever his Jewish workers were threatened, he brainstormed new strategies to keep them safe, even going so far as to bribe Nazi officials, move his factory to a new location, and send a subordinate to Auschwitz to bargain for the lives of his workers.

Emotional stability under pressure: Dr. Graham found that highly skilled drivers had the ability to maintain stability and continue with the task at hand, in spite of negative emotions such as fear, frustration, and anger. Although Oskar did have the occasional outburst, part of his success came from keeping a cool head under the extreme pressure he faced. Those who worked alongside him in those years say that he was at his best when under extreme pressure. Pressure seems to have been a source of stability for Oskar. People with Oskar's temperament easily handle situations that would cause others to crumble. Oskar thrived under pressure, but when unemployed, or simply bored, he was prone to depression, mood swings, and the destructive indulgence of alcohol. Mood disorders are quite common in people diagnosed with ADHD.

Oskar appears to have been suited for intensity. Modern research has been accumulating on this very topic and suggests that some people, like him, are just born with a built-in need for intense stimulus.[27] A study of skydivers, for example, found much in common between their positive thrill-seeking behaviors and the negative thrill-seeking of individuals struggling with addiction.[28] In both cases, there exists a strong need for exploratory behavior, novelty seeking, and risk taking.[29] What is most interesting is that certain variations of a dopamine transporter gene, such as the seven-repeat allele of the DRD4 gene, are found in a high percentage of thrill-seeking individuals, those with ADHD, and those who struggle with substance abuse. While much more research needs to be done, a compelling case can be made that thrill seeking is to some extent an innate trait.

Oskar had a need for speed. Evidence continues to build that some types of ADHD correlate with genes that involve novelty seeking.[30] Some individuals, like Oskar, exhibit a drive for exhilaration. If they cannot get this "need" met positively, they will find a way to negatively create the intensity they crave. This tendency can easily be viewed as a character flaw, but harnessed in a positive way, it could well be an evolutionary advantage. Some scientists think that some of what we consider ADHD symptoms, like rapidly shifting focus and quick movements, are actually survival traits that were common among those humans who initially chose to migrate out of Africa.[31] People who decided to go on that dangerous trek and populate the rest of the world tens of thousands of years ago were obviously explorers and risk-takers. When you take someone whose brain is wired for risk-taking and adventure and put him or her in situation of monotony and boredom, bad things usually happen.

Oskar usually managed to find thrills, but for most of his life, these were of a negative, destructive, and careless nature. He lost jobs, businesses, piles of money, and his marriage. As Ned Hallowell has pointed out, Oskar had a "race car brain built with bicycle brakes." The race-car orientation of his brain, nevertheless, allowed him to perform some amazing feats of courageous compassion.

Did Oskar Truly Have ADHD?

An ADHD diagnosis requires that an individual meet at list six of nine characteristics in one or both symptom clusters, *primarily inattentive* and *hyperactive-impulsive*. Also, impairment needs to have been present early in life and must exist in multiple areas. Psychologists make a diagnosis by testing the individual, as well as distributing questionnaires to teachers

18

and parents in the case of a child, or a spouse, in the case of an adult. Such testing did not exist in Oskar's day, but the evidence for Oskar having ADHD is simply overwhelming; his life reads like a case study of ADHD in a graduate psychology class. Consider the following ADHD traits, taken from questionnaires that are routinely used in diagnosis. Much overlap exists between traits; this is not a full list of ADHD symptoms.

1. Fails to give close attention to details or makes careless mistakes in schoolwork, work, or other activities. Oskar started many businesses. The evidence is strong and consistent that he got excited at the idea of starting a business but failed in handling the details. Once when his wife Emilie was out of town, he even failed to take care of their dog, who subsequently died as a result. His wife called him "habitually inattentive." This point leads to another trait examined to diagnose an adult with ADHD:

2. Does not follow through on instructions and fails to finish duties in the workplace. Steven Spielberg captured these traits in *Schindler's List* in a dialogue between Oskar and Yitzhak Stern.

> Yitzhak Stern: Let me understand. They put up all the money. I do all the work. What, if you don't mind my asking, would you do?

> Oskar Schindler: I'd make sure it's known the company's in business. I'd see that it had a certain panache. That's what I'm good at. Not the work, not the work: The presentation.[32]

Oskar was brilliant at making friends and creating excitement, but another ADHD trait prevented him from using these abilities to ultimately succeed. Incidentally, it was when I saw the above scene in the movie that I started to wonder if Oskar had ADHD.

3. Difficulty organizing tasks and activities. He had great ideas but struggled to see the logical steps he needed to follow to carry those out. One of his get-rich-quick schemes involved raising nutria, beaver-like rodents, for making fur coats. He told his wife: "Emilie, behold before you the business of the century. We're going to be millionaires. All the women wear fur coats."[33] Emilie ended up doing all the work in this venture because her "husband was always busy elsewhere."[34] Oskar had a tendency to flit from one brilliant idea to the next. After he completely lost interest in the nutria business, he left Emilie in Argentina to run the operation and sought his fortune elsewhere. He set sail for Germany almost without warning, a pattern of wanderlust that he exhibited his whole life.[35] It is appropriate, therefore, to diagnose Oskar with another important factor in ADHD.

4. Restlessness. He never stayed in one job or place very long. Oh, he must have had a hard time sitting in a desk in school all day. His time in Kraków during World War II represented the most geographically stable period of his adult life. Even at that time, though, he frequently traveled for business and pleasure. Staying in one place, or staying on one task, was a great challenge for Oskar Schindler.

5. Oskar also avoided tasks that required sustained mental effort. He was imaginative and creative, but the daily grind got to him. Oskar relied on an army of Jewish workers to handle the details of his businesses. "Give me the summary," he frequently told them. "I don't need the minutiae."[36] Oskar's wife and associates have all described his inability to stay on the same topic or same task for long.

ADHD people, like Oskar, have a wide attentional focus. They naturally pay attention to more of the stimuli around them than the average person. ADHD people do not filter out information, which makes them much more easily distractible,

20

but there is also a positive side to this. The more elements activated in one's attentional "stream" opens up greater possibility of arriving at a more unique mixing of elements and consequently more original ideas.[37] The expanded attentional focus and consequent distractibility associated with ADHD gives a person an advantage in specific aspects of creative thinking, such as those that call for ignoring an immediate context and being open to other, perhaps creative, contexts.[38] This ability, incidentally, is also crucial in telling jokes, another skill Oskar excelled at.

6. Oskar had difficulty sustaining attention in many tasks, especially those he found boring. Novelty, intensity, and excitement roused Oskar and brought out his inner genius, but once a task or endeavor became routine or repetitive, Schindler lacked the ability to continue plodding. This tendency was present in his work, relationships, and of course had appeared early in school.

7. Oskar was often forgetful in daily activities. Many of the Jews who worked in the administration of Oskar's operation assumed he would forget, and they frequently reminded him of important duties. During the war, Oskar bragged that he could leave his business for weeks at a time in the hands of Abraham Bankier, his business manager.[39] Without Bankier, many observers have said, Oskar's operation would have completely fallen apart.

8. Oskar was described as someone of very high energy, hyperactive, as if driven by a motor. It is not difficult to imagine that school, as mentioned above, would have been a struggle. I have no trouble envisioning Oskar interrupting teachers, making snide remarks, and excessively talking, all traits one would see in a high-energy ADHD youngster. A man who was described as always on the go, loud and boisterous, and always looking for something "new" and "exciting" would today certainly be suspected of having ADHD.

How then was this man with so much difficulty in life able to rise to an extraordinary level of heroism? This question is answered easily and poetically in these lines spoken in the movie by Liam Neeson, who played Schindler:

> Oskar Schindler: In every business I tried, I can see now, it wasn't me that failed. Something was missing. Even if I'd known what it was, there's nothing I could have done about it because you can't create this thing. And it makes all the difference in the world between success and failure.
>
> Emilie Schindler: Luck?
>
> Oskar Schindler: War![40]

The intensity of the war years put so much pressure on Oskar that they allowed the diamond of his genius and true nature to emerge in full splendor.

Raising Schindler

If you have a child, loved one, or friend like Oskar Schindler, this chapter should kick off a process of reimagining his or her life.

☐ Failure in school DOES NOT ALWAYS lead to failure in life. There are many who use their challenges to grow. Put up posters around your home or office of famous people with ADHD or who were unique, different learners. Some examples include: Thomas Edison, Katherine Ellison, Leonardo DaVinci, Vincent Van Gogh, Oskar Schindler, and Michael Phelps. Shift your mindset and relentlessly focus on the positives.

☐ A need to move and use one's hands is not bad! Find ways to engage the hands-on nature of your loved one. Take nature hikes; find a sport that he or she loves; build things together; take things apart together. Integrate movement into learning. When I get stuck in writing, for example, I take a brisk walk and talk out my ideas into a tape recorder. Some of my best ideas, including this "Raising Schindler" section, come when I am on a walk.

☐ Make sure that teachers understand the type of individual they are dealing with and take them to task when you feel they are pathologizing your loved one's nature. Have a *zero tolerance* attitude for anyone who causes your loved one to feel bad about him or herself!

☐ Unique individuals often have extraordinary skills that school neither honors nor helps to cultivate. Take care to recognize, support, and develop these skills. Like Schindler, your loved one might have uncommon empathy, a great imagination, a love of mechanical things, or maybe the ability to craft stories. Had Schindler not been a great storyteller, he probably would not have been able to outwit the Nazis. Help your loved one find his or her strengths and be always on the lookout for opportunities to develop them. Make this a primary goal.

☐ While different learners and people with ADHD may struggle in school, they often excel in pursuits that involve adventure or risk-taking, and that require creativity and imagination. Geo-caching can help positively meet this need, along with adventure bike rides, hunting, rocketry, robotics, camping, fishing, hiking, playing paint ball, or intensive exploration near home (Teach safety first!).

☐ People like Oskar Schindler NEED intensity. If we fail to find positive ways of meeting this need, negative paths will be pursued. Realize that the unconscious drive to seek out intensity can lead to arguments, impulsive actions, and a whole host of negativity-producing behaviors. One of your most important tasks is to cultivate a mindset that understands the brain-driven differences in your loved one so that you do not take his or her negative behaviors personally. You have to find a calm harbor of balance within yourself that allows you to respond instead of reacting. Meditation, mindfulness training, and yoga can be of great benefit in this pursuit. You cannot just will yourself to change; you have to get support and guidance and make such activities a daily practice. Please do not use this book, incidentally, as a substitute for professional help and consultation.

☐ The world's greatest minds usually suffer under the narrow rules of school. Flip your thinking pattern and see trouble in school not as a problem but as a sign of a potentially brilliant future.

NOTES

1 This conversation between Emilie and Oskar, like many interchanges between the couple featured in this book, comes from sources close to the couple, and in many cases I have taken literary license to help create a more flowing narrative. I have taken great pains to ensure that any conversations depicted in this work conform to the authentic character of these two remarkable individuals, and in most cases the lines you read are based on lines actually uttered by the people you will read about in this book. I have used dozens of sources, including the writings of Emilie Schindler, statements by family friends and acquaintances, as well as numerous documents of Schindler survivors that give testimony to their lives. I have heavily relied on Robin O'Neil, David Crowe and Mietek Pemper as well, in addition to combing through numerous interviews of Schindler survivors and Oskar Schindler himself. I have had phone conversations with Crowe and O'Neil, and made use of historical archives in Kraków and Auschwitz in Poland. One very special conversation took place between myself and Dr. Joseph Biederman, one of the major authorities on ADHD, whose parents were both saved by Oskar Schindler. Dr. Biederman met Oskar Schindler and, like many Schindler survivors, his parents gave direct assistance to Oskar after the war. Without Schindler, the Biederman's would not have survived and the world would have been deprived of one of its great advocates and researchers into ADHD.

1 • *The Oskars of the World*

2 Ibid.

3 Ibid.

4 Ibid.

5 O'Neill, R. (2010). *Oskar Schindler, Stepping Stone to Life.* Robin O'Neill: United Kingdom. Crowe, D. (2004). *Oskar Schindler: The Untold Account of his Life, Wartime Activities, and the true story behind the List.* Basic Books: New York. These two authors, along with Mietek Pemper, have served as my main sources.

6 O'Neil.

7 Crowe, 4.

8 Crowe, 3.

9 Corroborated by Crowe and O'Neil, although this quote is not direct.

10 Hanc, T., Brzezinska, A. (2009). Intensity of ADHD Symptoms and Subjective Feelings of Competence in School Age Children. *School Psychology International,* Vol. 30, Issue 5.

11 O'Neil.

12 Honigsfeld, A., & Dunn, R. (2009). Learning-Style Responsive Approaches for Teaching, *Clearing House,* Vol. 82, Issue 6.

13 Roucek, J. (1940). Czechoslovakia and Her Minorities. In R. Kerner (Ed.), *Czechoslovakia* (pp. 171-192), Berkeley, CA: University of California Press.

14 Russell, J. (1899). *German Higher Schools.* New York, NY: Longmans, Green, and Co.

Paulsen, F. (1908). *German Education Past and Present,* London, England: T Fisher Unwin.

15 Paulsen.

16 Gatto, J.T. (2003). The public school nightmare, *Library of Halexandria.* Online. Available at http://www.halexandria.org/dward036.htm.

17 Miller, A. (1990). *For Your Own Good: Hidden Cruelty in Child-Rearing and the Roots of Violence* (3rd ed.). Farrar, Straus & Giroux.

18 Crowe, 3-4.

19 Roberts, K. (2012). *Movers, Dreamers, and Risk-Takers: Unlocking the Power of ADHD.* Center City, MN: Hazelden.

20 O'Neil.

21 Crowe.

22 Ibid.

23 Crowe and O'Neil.

24 Crowe, 6-7.

25 Graham, D. (1987). The Racer's Edge: a Strong Psyche. *New York Times*, 24 May.

26 *Schindler's List*. Dir. Steven Spielberg. 1993. Universal Pictures. DVD.

27 Myrseth, E., Tverå, R., Hagatun., S. & Lindgren, C. (2012). A comparison of impulsivity and sensation seeking in pathological gamblers and skydivers. *Scandinavian Journal of Psychology*.

28 Ibid.

29 Matthews, L., & Butler, P. (2011). Novelty-seeking DRD4 polymorphisms are associated with human migration distance out-of-Africa after controlling for neutral population gene structure, *American Journal of Physical Anthropology*, Vol. 145, Issue 3.

30 Kebir, K. Tabbane, S. Sengupta, and Joober, R. (2009). Candidate genes and neuropsychological phenotypes in children with ADHD: Review of Association Studies, *Journal of Psychiatry and Neuroscience*, Vol. 34, Issue 2: 88–101. Yang, M., Ishii, J., McCracken, J., McGough, J., Loo, S., Nelson, S., Smalley, S. (2005). Temperament and character profiles and the dopamine D4 receptor gene in ADHD. *American Journal of Psychiatry*, Vol. 162, Issue 5.

31 Myrseth et al.

32 *Schindler's List*. Dir. Steven Spielberg. 1993. Universal Pictures. DVD.

33 Schindler, E. & Rosenberg, E. (1996). *Where Light and Shadow Meet* (Trans. D. Koch). New York: W.W. Norton and Company, p. 127.

34 Schindler, E., p. 128.

35 Schindler, E.

36 This line and ones similar to it have been verified by numerous sources.

37 Abraham, A., Windmann, S., Siefen, R., Daum, I., & Güntürkün, O. (2006). Creative Thinking in Adolescents with Attention Deficit Hyperactivity Disorder (**ADHD**). *Child Neuropsychology*, Vol. 12, Issue 2.

38 Ibid.

39 Pemper, O'Neil, Crowe.

40 *Schindler's List*. Dir. Steven Spielberg. 1993. Universal Pictures. DVD.

Chapter 2 Wine, Women, and War

Schindler was a drunkard. Schindler was a womanizer.
Everything he did put him in jeopardy. If Schindler had been
a normal man, he would not have done what he did.

—Mosche Bejski, Schindler Survivor,
and Israeli Supreme Court Justice

Destined for Failure

SCHINDLER CONSTANTLY MEASURED his achievements against a persistent and nagging inner voice: "You will never amount to anything, Oskar."[1] That toxic refrain came from his father, and it played in his head, even at the heights of success. When he won his first motorcycle race, his father came up and said as he patted him on the back, "Well, you won, Oskar. How long before you move on to something new?" Oskar was well aware that he had trouble sticking with anything for very long, but his father made this sort of remark frequently, cutting into him, leaving a deep emotional gash that never quite healed. His father's unremitting disapproval was just one of many things that made Oskar feel different, like he would never be able to measure up. "I've always felt different deep inside myself,"[2] Oskar told Emilie and close friends.

27

I can tell you from personal and professional experience that most ADHDers, like Oskar, feel abnormal and struggle with that their whole lives. ADHD people approach almost everything in life—school, work, sports, and relationships—in an atypical manner. As a consequence, we skirt the margins of society, which can make us perfect out-of-the-box thinkers, endowed with the gifts of imagination and creative thought. ADHD does make it difficult, however, to use those gifts in positive, consistent, and productive ways; of that, there can be no doubt. Oskar teemed with talent and brilliant ideas, but he struggled to accomplish or finish anything. Being constantly reminded of that by his father served not to motivate him, but to fill Oskar with lifelong self-doubt.

Hans Schindler, Oskar's father, was not just guilty of snide remarks towards his son. "He was a nasty, nasty man," Emilie said, "and luckily he travelled a lot because we were always glad to have him gone."[3] He was a heavy drinker and serially cheated on Oskar's mother, an example that the son was to follow. The elder Schindler was prone to frequent emotional outbursts and hurled insults at family members as a matter of daily habit, especially when under the influence of alcohol. Hans created mayhem wherever he went. Emilie Schindler despised him. Her recollections of Hans are all of a disturbing nature:

> Suddenly my father-in-law stumbled into the house, totally drunk, carrying in one hand a cake and with the other holding on to any support he could find along his way. He noticed my look of disapproval—for that he was sober enough—and when he was about to say something to me, I cut him off. He was furious, and since he could not throw me out, he kicked my dog out of the house while repeating over and over, in his drunken babble, that animals belonged on the street.[4]

Oskar grew up with a man who was abusive along with being an alcoholic. Research has shown higher levels of stress, difficulty with life's challenges, and more symptoms of personal dysfunction in adult children of alcoholics,[5] although there is wide variance in these behaviors. Oskar exhibited several characteristics that research has strongly associated with people who grew up in an alcoholic home. Some of these actually overlap with his ADHD symptoms. Adult children of alcoholics…

- Have difficulty following a project through from beginning to end.
- Lie when it would be just as easy to tell the truth.
- Have difficulty with intimate relationships.
- Usually feel they are different from other people.
- Are super responsible or super irresponsible (Oskar exhibited both of these).
- Are impulsive.
- Constantly seek approval and affirmation.[6]

Oskar did not exhibit just a few of these traits; he exhibited all of them. This is completely understandable, and even predictable: Oskar was born into a family environment and with a genetic heritage that put him at great risk for substance abuse and antisocial behavior. ADHD and substance abuse comprise a difficult duo, making life infinitely more challenging. Oskar was born with potent barriers to success and happiness.

Oskar's genetic inheritance certainly gave him a predisposition toward ADHD and alcoholism, but events in his family life and experiences in school played a crucial role in his difficulties as well.[8] Some ADHD people go on to develop an antisocial orientation, one characterized by deep-seated opposition to authority and a lack of concern for the norms of society. Chaos and conflict within the family are strongly associated with the eventual development of these very troublesome mindsets. Oskar exhibited antisocial traits by the time of his adolescence and as a result, had a very rough start in life. I do not think he ever fully dealt with his tendency toward defiance and his unwillingness to "play by the rules." A clinical psychologist who examined Oskar today would certainly screen him for Conduct Disorder, as well as Oppositional Defiant Disorder. ADHD and a family history of substance abuse are strongly associated with other behavioral disorders.

Breaking the Law

"People from that area," Emilie said, "saw Oskar as a con man, even a thief. He was not considered an ordinary, regular person."[9] From the age of sixteen, Oskar enjoyed renown, or should I say infamy, in the town of Svitavy for his chain smoking and regular attendance at the local pubs and bars.[10] His mother tried to get him to change his ways. "You're going to end up just like your father,"[11] she told him the morning after his sixteenth birthday when he had come home and passed out drunk. "This is how he started, Oskar. Bars are a gateway to suffering, nothing more." Oskar paid her no mind, but objected to her insinuation: "I am nothing like my father, nor will I ever be," he insisted. "I am going to succeed and show him just how wrong he is about me."[12] His mother replied, "Oskar, he's the failure. He gets on you because he isn't man enough to get on himself. People in this town thought he was destined for great success, but he has not lived up to those expectations. Every bad thing he says about you he really means about himself. You've got to understand that and stop destroying your chances for success."[13] Oskar did not see his own behavior as destructive. "I feel alive when I am at the pub," he told his mother. "It bustles with fun, excitement, and even a little play-

Oskar's Genes

ADHD and alcoholism have a significant association with variations in certain dopamine transporter and receptor genes[7] that we have already briefly touched on, as well as many other gene variants. I have not examined Oskar's genome, but if we were to discover a testable piece of his DNA, I am certain we would find many genetic variants associated with both ADHD and alcoholism. Incidentally, ADHD is a polygenic (many genes) condition; no single gene "gives" a person ADHD. Many genes combine.

ADHD, alcoholism, and an abusive home life made three strikes against Oskar. He went into life with terrible psychological, genetic, and neurobiological handicaps. As we will see, some of these handicaps made it easier for him to mingle with the antisocial brutes of the Gestapo and SS.

ful mischief. I need that. It's one of the only times I feel fully alive."

That feeling of *aliveness* could have had something to do with Oskar's involvement in barroom brawls, which got him arrested on numerous occasions. The police and judges in Svitavy knew him well,[14] and again, his peers called him "Schindler the swindler." If Oskar were going through adolescence nowadays, he would receive regular and frequent M.I.P.s (minor in possession citations) and probably be on constant probation, and he would maybe even end up in juvenile detention. With our society's burgeoning penchant for incarceration, a modern-day Oskar would be at a substantial risk of doing stints behind bars.

Between 1931 and 1938, Oskar racked up six convictions on his criminal record. Five of these were for fighting and assault. In one instance in 1938, he was charged with making dangerous threats, swindling, and fighting.[15] He was convicted and spent two months in jail. People who knew Oskar confirmed there were many other criminal charges during this period, but only a handful can be corroborated with documentation. It must be remembered that this region was badly damaged during World War II, and many records were lost. According to one court record that was located several decades after the war, Oskar was accused in 1933 of "theft in company" and was incarcerated from February 17 to March 21.[16] Records indicate that the case was sent up to a higher court, but the final disposition of the matter cannot be determined. What can be determined, however, is that Schindler regularly broke the law, and getting caught did not deter him from further violations.

Oskar exhibited a pattern, like most ADHDers, of acting impulsively for short-term gain without possessing actionable awareness of the long-term consequences, which could have tempered his behavior. Many, if not most, of his business dealings can be accurately assessed as get-rich-quick schemes because he was out for a hurried and hefty payoff for a minimal amount of work. In fact, when he left his home in 1939 to seek his fortune in Poland, he hoped to get rich in record time and then disappear with a "steamer trunk full of money."[17]

Oskar was a gambler, willing to risk everything for a slight, perhaps infinitesimally small, chance at fabulous wealth. Gambling not only characterized his business dealings, but he also regularly bet and lost large amounts of money playing cards and shooting dice. When he married his wife, Emilie, her father gave the couple a very generous present. "My father gifted us 100,000 Czech crowns," Emilie said, "which was a virtual fortune in those days. We could have had a beautiful house with that money or even bought a business, but Oskar quickly squandered every penny. He bought a luxury car, went on lavish drinking binges, and just had to gamble, which he was not, incidentally, very good at."[18] He had an easy-come-easy-go attitude with money and was always looking for the "next big score." Emilie's attempts to encourage moderation and thrift in Oskar were always dismissed and even characterized with contempt: "Emilie, you are too austere, a real ascetic. While, on the other hand, I am by nature a sybarite."[19] Oskar's favorite ancient Greek city, Sybaris, was so incredibly rich that the name became synonymous with the quest of extreme wealth and pleasure, pursuits he admired. Oskar's inability to tolerate routines, perform mundane tasks, and follow through on details ensured that for most of his life, his sybaritic longings went unfulfilled for lack of money; when he did have money, he quickly gambled it away.

Compulsive gambling is, incidentally, seen much more frequently in ADHD individuals.[20] The circuits of the brain involved in controlling impulses are especially crucial in this condition.[21] In people like Oskar who have problems with alcohol, the inability to inhibit the impulse to gamble seems to get worse over time.[22] This explains to some extent the fact that Oskar showed increasing imprudence in his business dealings after the war. His hair-brained money-making ideas started to look less like business ventures and more like outright crap shoots.

The Lady's Man

Oskar courted multiple women at a time and had an insatiable sex drive. His relationship with sex, like so many other things in his life, was decidedly impulsive and addictive. He was sexually active from a very young age, which—with the lack of consciousness around birth control at that time—had serious consequences. By the time he was nineteen, before he married

Impulsivity in the Brain

Impulsivity, acting without thinking, is a behavior with strong correlates to differences in the brain. One brain region, the caudate nucleus, is strongly associated with impulsivity. People with no history of impulsivity who experience trauma to this area of the frontal part of the brain become impulsive.[23] Many irregularities have been uncovered in the size and shape of this cerebral region in ADHD boys, though not in girls, with which there are several gene variant correlations. Given Oskar's behavior, it is highly probable that he had an irregularly shaped, atypically functioning caudate nucleus.

In ADHD people, the brain networks responsible for self-management, emotional control, and self-regulation develop later than in the non-ADHD population.[24] Further, in some people with ADHD, these networks never fully mature. Even when the brains of people with ADHD do "catch up," the negative messages that resulted from impulsivity and poor choices persist. The greatest side effect of an ADHD diagnosis is the long-term damage to self-esteem.

Emilie, he had fathered twins,[25] a fact no one knew until after his death in 1974. Further revelations revealed two additional children out of wedlock.[26] People with ADHD, incidentally, have a much higher rate of out-of-wedlock births, which is why today many adopted children have ADHD; in other words, people with ADHD are more likely to have unwanted pregnancies, and thus statistically, children who are adopted are more genetically predisposed to having ADHD.

Had Oskar been more of a self-reflective individual, he may have realized that marriage and fatherhood were incompatible with his lifestyle. From the very day of the wedding, the union between Oskar and Emilie seemed doomed to failure. The police had received credible information that Schindler was already married. They arrested and detained him and investigated the matter; it turned out that Schindler had been living for over three years with a woman much older than he, a fact he had hidden from his new wife. "The allegation of bigamy was malicious, but the facts were correct and caused Emilie much heartache. She never forgave him."[27] In spite of this inauspicious start, the Schindlers stayed together for over thirty years, quite a feat considering Oskar's constant and vigorous infidelity.

Oskar exhibited both an inability to form long-lasting romantic intimacy and cruelty towards his wife. As I have examined the record, my esteem for Oskar has diminished when I consider how poorly he treated Emilie, which stands in stark contrast to her constancy and forgiveness. On the other hand, his behavior as a husband demonstrates the depth of Oskar's psychological wounds. I say this not to excuse his actions, but to understand them. Oskar needed to be in therapy and probably would have benefited from medication, meditation, and mindfulness training. He received no treatment for ADHD or addiction, living at a time when the understanding of both conditions was at best in its infancy.

Coming from a family that dealt with infidelity, alcoholism, and frequent fighting, Oskar did not have a good model to follow. Oskar did not seek treatment, and again there wasn't much available, so his emotional scars persisted. Coupled with an adventure-driven and addictive-oriented sexuality, he sought superficial satisfaction from a stream of women rather than doing the difficult work of confronting the demons from the past that prevented him from succeeding as a long-term partner. In many ways, his relationship to women bore striking similarity to his relationship to business: initial enthusiasm followed by disillusionment and boredom, which led him to frequently flee to find new excitement. Obviously, this tendency can also be viewed through the ADHD lens: When stimuli become boring or routine, the ADHD brain becomes less active. Therefore, in an effort to reactivate and reinvigorate the brain, new stimulation is sought out. For this, among many reasons, ADHD-ers often experience relationship difficulties.

The fact that ADHD people are always *shifting* attention results from an unconscious need to bring in new stimulation,[28] a reality governed by differences in the ADHD brain. Brain imaging, for example, shows that certain parts of the ADHD brain are underactive in certain low-stimuli situations.[29] EEG scans show excessive slow-wave activity in the ADHD brain,[30] and poor functioning in the parts of brain known to play a role in planning, organization, motivation, and impulse control, which are, generally, called executive functions. Oskar was always seeking out new stimuli in an effort, like all ADHDers, to unconsciously compensate for an underactive and atypically functioning brain. Again, when stimuli lose their novelty and become mundane and boring, the ADHD brain often does not work well.[31] This is scientific truth. During World War II, Oskar did not have to work hard to activate his ADHD brain: adventure and excitement came to him, a fact that helps account for his epic deeds at that time.

From Darkness ... Light

The years leading up to the Second World War were not good to Oskar. He served in the Czechoslovak army, worked in customer service, found employment as a salesman, and tried his hand at poultry farming, an endeavor at which he miserably failed. Farming, incidentally, involves repeated plodding, something most ADHD people find synonymous with suffering. Oskar yearned for adventure and had nothing engaging to hold his interest. "Emile, I feel I was made for some grand undertaking, one worthy of my energy and skills," he told her on numerous occasions. "Something just seems missing. I have never found the true challenge I was meant to take up."[32] Such talk scared Emilie, because she knew just how prone Oskar was to taking huge and dangerous risks. "Sometimes, great challenges are achieved by taking small steps every single day," she tried to tell him. "And then those small steps add up to something big."[33] Baby steps were never going to work for Oskar Schindler. He wanted it all, and he wanted it now, but by the late 1930s, this attitude led to the Schindlers having nothing, except a great deal of marital stress.

His charming nature kept his marriage going, but he persisted with the pattern of debauchery and recklessness. Unemployment led to boredom. "You have nothing to do," Emilie tried to reason with him, "and that always means you will get bored, which you, Oskar, cannot tolerate. You will find something exciting, but incredibly stupid, to get out of that boredom, and bring shame on yourself and your family in the process."[34] In spite of Emilie's calm reasoning, Oskar followed a predictable cycle of acting out and then begging her for forgiveness. For Emilie, this was one of the most disconcerting aspects of his personality:

> In spite of his flaws, Oskar had a big heart and was always ready to help whoever was in need. He was affable, kind, extremely generous, and charitable, but at the same time, not mature at all. He constantly lied and deceived me, and later returned feeling sorry, like a boy caught in mischief asking to be forgiven one more time.... And then we would start all over again.[35]

Oskar was a big kid who never fully grew up. ADHD and alcoholism did not help that process, as both conditions are known to impede psychological growth. ADHDers struggle developmentally, academically, socially, and emotionally. The events of the 1930s lent a hand to Oskar's stunted development. In the fiery furnace of Europe on the eve of World War II, a strange alchemy began to work in the life of Oskar Schindler. His vices steadily shifted from being the agents of failure to the raw materials of success. Without his womanizing, gambling, excessive drinking, constant boredom, restlessness, and reckless spirit of adventure, close to twelve hundred more Jewish people would have perished in the Holocaust and thousands more would never have been born. An individual who had actively sought out danger and intrigue would find himself awash in so much intensity that he was able to steadfastly persist in one endeavor for several years, an aptitude that eluded him thereafter. His dark side provided him with the requisite skills to navigate some of the most troubled waters humanity has ever encountered.

Dark Clouds

To understand the pressure that helped the humanitarian genius of Oskar Schindler emerge, we have to appreciate the dark clouds that had begun to hang over Europe. Oskar was a Sudeten German living in Czechoslovakia. While people from his ethnic group had ultimately managed to do relatively well in the newly formed country, there was still an undercurrent of dissatisfaction. They considered themselves German, after all, and resentment of the Czechoslovak government lay just under the surface. When Adolph Hitler came to power in Germany in early 1933, the "virus of National Socialism struck the Sudeten Germans."[36] In that same year, they formed the Sudeten German Party under the leadership of Konrad

Poster urging support for the annexation of the Sudenten-
land, 1938. *United States Holocaust Memorial Museum, courtesy of
Galerie Prospect*

Henlein, a pro-German Nazi sympathizer. He told his followers that he refused to let Sudeten Germans be treated as
second-class citizens. The Führer, German for "leader," was on
their side and would lend assistance.[37] In 1935, Henlein started
to receive significant sums of money from the German government. This coupling between the Sudeten Germans and the

Nazis was a driving force in Europe's march toward war. Hitler skillfully manipulated the Sudeten German situation to help justify German expansionism.

Partly with Nazi support, the Sudeten German Party captured 60 percent of the Sudeten German vote in the 1935 elections.[38] Henlein, the Sudetenland's *Hitler*, proposed that the region be annexed to the German Reich.[39] It is with these developments in mind that we can begin to understand Oskar Schindler's support of this party and his affinity for the German Reich, or empire. Oskar was not an ideologue. He got caught up in a wave of pro-German sentiment and attached himself emotionally and politically to a country that was fast becoming the most powerful in Europe. Oskar, assisted by his internal demons, found his way into that cauldron of power.

In 1935, on one of his many adventurous weekends away from Emilie, Oskar Schindler had a romantic tryst with a woman named Amelia[40] who, just as much as anyone else in the story, was a linchpin in Oskar's success. "Oskar, I think you would like my new friends in Berlin,"[41] Amelia told him. "You are the kind of man they are looking for." Amelia, whom he first met in Kraków, worked for the German counterintelligence service and put in a good word for Oskar with her superiors.[42] This chance meeting is one of the events that eventually allowed Oskar to become an operative for German intelligence in Czechoslovakia and Poland.

A little over a year later, in 1937, Ilse Pelikanova, another of Oskar's female acquaintances, invited him to a lavish New Year's party in Berlin.[43] This seminal event allowed Oskar to mingle with and charm some of the highest ranking officers in the German army, the Wehrmacht, and the army intelligence service, the Abwehr. In fact, this party likely gave Oskar the opportunity to make the acquaintance of Admiral Wilhelm Canaris, head of German army intelligence and a man who had

Nazi Terminology

For the sake of clarity, below are a few German terms that will help you better understand the story.

Gestapo: This word is an abbreviation of Geheime Staatspolizei, which was the secret police that operated in Germany and Nazi-occupied lands. This organization had enormous power to arrest, detain, and even murder enemies of the Nazi state. The Gestapo spread terror throughout Europe.

Wehrmacht: This word simply means the German regular army.

Abwehr: This organization was the military-intelligence wing of the German army. Many Nazi leaders became suspicious of the Abwehr because it did not exhibit the anti-Semitism that the Nazis so vigorously enforced.

SS: The SS, short for Schutzstaffel, was a paramilitary force set up as the vanguard of Nazi values. It contained some of the most brutal and anti-Semitic Nazis. Their belief in Nazi ideals was close to religious zeal. Incidentally, Schutzstaffel means "protective squad," and this group provided protection, in the early days, at Nazi party rallies. Its leader was Heinrich Himmler.

Sicherheitsdienst: This was another intelligence-gathering organization, but unlike the Abwehr, its members possessed a very anti-Semitic and brutal mindset. It was something of a sister organization of the Gestapo. Its leader was Reinhard Heydrich, a man most admired and highly respected by Hitler.

access to Hitler himself. Charming the admiral at the party, Oskar made a friend whose influence was later to help him out of many scrapes with fervent Nazis, the Gestapo, and various agencies of the SS. Although Oskar initially resisted becoming a full member of the Abwehr, another woman with whom Oskar had a long romantic relationship, Gritt Schwarzer, convinced him later that year to serve Germany.[44]

Oskar had gained entry, via the multiple women in his life, to the upper echelon of power in the German government. He quickly became a go-to guy for information on the Sudetenland, and he was particularly useful because of his facility with languages. He happened to live in the corridor of territory most coveted by Hitler and spoke, to varying degrees, many of the languages of the countries Hitler hoped to soon bend to his will.

Hitler had come to power in 1933 with an expressed commitment to return Germany to its former glory. He and his followers believed that Germany had lost World War I, and had gone into economic collapse, because of a worldwide Jewish conspiracy. From the very outset of his political activities, he believed it was Germany's destiny to expand its borders and to rule over what he considered the lesser races of human beings. These included Jews, Gypsies, and Slavic peoples, like those in Oskar's homeland of Czechoslovakia and its neighbor next door, Poland. Time and again, Hitler claimed that Germany was hemmed in and needed living space, or *Lebensraum*, an idea that in Hitler's mind justified his expansionist agenda. Oskar Schindler assisted the Germans in gathering information that would make it easier to destroy Poland and Czechoslovakia and thus add these countries to the Third Reich. As Hitler stated in *Mein Kampf*,

> Without consideration of "traditions" and prejudices, it [Germany] must find the courage to gather our people and their strength for an advance along the road that will lead this people from its present re-

stricted living space to new land and soil, and hence also free it from the danger of vanishing from the earth or of serving others as a slave nation.[45]

Hitler's goals could not have been articulated more clearly. In his worldview, millions of other people would need to vanish from Earth in order for Germans to prosper.

Oskar became swept up by the wave of German nationalism that rumbled in the Sudeten part of Czechoslovakia, a wave that promised to bring Hitler's ideas to fruition. Interviews with Czechoslovak authorities, however, suggest that his interest in spying had a lot to do with his desire to make money as well. He seemed to thrive in the danger and excitement of espionage, but much of the intrigue unsettled Emilie. Their lives were under frequent surveillance, and Emilie lived in constant fear. Not only was she forced to move from her hometown, but the thin threads of stability she previously held had completely vanished. On one occasion, she returned from a trip to discover their home had been ransacked:

> I found our apartment in shambles: clothes out of their drawers, papers strewn all over the floor, broken lamps, a truly devastating sight. The only sound to be heard was that of a telephone, off the hook and thrown on the floor, under a layer of clothes, torn papers, busted pillows and feathers, shards from porcelain vases and dishes that apparently had been thrown furiously against the walls by our desperate visitors, frustrated because they did not find any of the things they had supposedly come for.[46]

While every job he had ever held made him frustrated and bored, espionage held the power to firmly focus Oskar's attention.

Treason and Death Sentence

In March 1938, Hitler's expansionist goals started to become reality. That month, Germany annexed Austria into the Third Reich. This bold event, known in German as the *Anschluss*, whipped Oskar and his fellow Czechoslovak Germans into frenzy. "They have Austria now," Oskar told Emilie with excitement, "and they will soon have Czeckoslovakia. Germany is now the most powerful nation in the world and we will soon be part of the greater, glorious German Reich."[47] Clear-headed Emilie was neither taken in by Hitler nor Henlein. "They scare me, Oskar," she told him repeatedly. "All this talk of the Jews. I fear Hitler and Henlein are up to no good."[48] Characteristically, Oskar tried to reassure her: "You worry too much. Hitler's not going to harm the Jews. The rest of the world would not stand for it. But he will help us. I really believe it."[49]

Those who supported him certainly did initially benefit from Hitler's favor. After taking over Austria, Nazi sympathizers occupied all positions of power in that nation. Hitler then set his sights next on Schindler's home region, the Sudetenland of Czechoslovakia, and Germany called on Oskar to assist. Hitler and his propaganda apparatus concocted a narrative that the Sudeten Germans were being mistreated by the Czechoslovak government. Hitler fashioned himself as the savior of this *oppressed* people.

In July 1938, Oskar was formally employed by the Abwehr, though he had by that point already been involved in espionage. His mission was to collect information on Czechoslovak transport networks, military installations, and troop movements. "You are now formally working for the Fatherland," Major von Korab of the Abwehr, told Oskar. "You are a true German patriot. With your help, the German army can swoop in before the Czechoslovak government even knows what's happening."[50] Pumped up with German propaganda and a true desire to help his fellow Sudeten Germans, Oskar went enthusiastically to work. He had no training, however, and his espionage activities were uncovered by the Czechoslovak authorities within a few weeks. Like many ADHD people, Oskar loved a new challenge, but he went into it blindly, neither considering the best practices to follow nor reflecting on the potential consequences, let alone his complete lack of training. He started collecting information right in his hometown!

Everybody in that town at least knew of Oskar. So, when he began acting strangely and asking unusual questions, people took notice. "How many soldiers are garrisoned in the Svitavy area?"[51] Oskar asked Leo Pruscha,[52] a local police inspector. He asked another acquaintance who he knew had served in the army, "Do you know how many police officers in Svitavy are also army reservists?"[53] Schindler also questioned a few railroad workers about transportation networks and railroad traffic, and he queried dozens of local residents. The police immediately launched an investigation, which uncovered incriminating papers which clearly showed Oskar's spying activities.[54] Within a few weeks of beginning to spy for the German army, Oskar was arrested by Czechoslovak authorities, summarily convicted of treason, and sentenced to death.

Oskar got a second chance though. In October of that same year, Oskar was languishing in prison, awaiting his execution. Before Czechoslovak authorities could carry out the sentence, however, Nazi aggression intervened. The Czech-German nationalist, Konrad Henlein, had conspired with Adolf Hitler. Henlein had received increased funding that year from Hitler to escalate the activity of Henlein's paramilitary group, the Sudeten Frei Corps. This group was tasked by Hitler with stirring up disturbances and clashes with the Czechoslovak government. The idea was to create the perception that the Sudeten Germans were being mistreated so that Hitler could swoop in and save them, thus "justifying" Nazi

aggression as simply a benevolent attempt to protect a perse-
cuted group of Germans.

As he awaited execution, Oskar's homeland became the
flashpoint of Europe, as Hitler seemed intent on marching
into Czechoslovakia to *protect* the Sudeten Germans. With
the threat of war, the European powers hastily organized the
Munich Conference, hoping to resolve the situation. Britain
and France wanted at all costs to avoid another world war.
They had, after all, suffered millions of casualties during World
War I and had no appetite for more of that. They were guided
by appeasement, the notion that they could preserve peace by
giving in to some of Hitler's unreasonable demands. There was,
it must be remembered, no real crisis, other than the one that
Hitler had craftily created. Germany was given the go-ahead at
Munich by Britain and France to annex the Sudetenland, and
as part of the deal, political prisoners, like Oskar Schindler,
were released. Many in Europe naïvely believed that peace had
been secured.

From that fortuitous event forward, Schindler began to
realize the type of life he had longed for, one filled with an
ever-increasing flow of new but perilous possibilities, excitement, and wild riches that he had only dreamed of. As
Hitler's Germany enjoyed success after success militarily,
Oskar's star started to shine brightly. "I was willing to die for
the Fatherland,"[55] he was fond of recounting. "And now the
Fatherland is going to provide for me."

German Agent

Under routine, repetitive, and predictable stimuli, ADHDers
like Oskar struggle to stay with one thing for very long. The war
years gave Oskar an inexhaustible reservoir of intensity. Every
minute of every day, Oskar had a flow of challenges that caused
the synaptic junctions of his brain to fire with astronomical
efficiency. In spite of the liabilities inherent in ADHD—lack

of follow through, trouble with planning and organization, maintaining prolonged focus—Oskar Schindler embarked on a seven-year run of success, fueled by circumstances that made most people want to flee. The very danger and horror that made others fear and suffer caused Oskar to excel.

The failure with ADHD became someone the German army held in high esteem, considering him a reliable and results-oriented operative. Just as Schindler had been involved in helping the German army in its pursuit to conquer the Sudetenland, he played a significant role in plans to take over Poland. Hitler wanted to make it appear that Poland was the aggressor, and to this end, leading SS figure Reinhard Heydrich, at Hitler's behest, arranged for a few dozen concentration camp prisoners to be shot while wearing Polish army uniforms near a German radio outpost on the Polish border.[56] Plans were carried out in cooperation with the Abwehr, under the command of Admiral Wilhelm Canaris, who, as will be discussed, counted Oskar Schindler as a friend.

As an Abwehr agent, Oskar was stationed after his release from prison on the Czech-Polish border in a spot called Moravska-Ostrava. Schindler employed agents to gather information about Polish transport networks, fortifications, and military installations, which was used as part of German military preparations to attack Poland. Acting on orders from his superiors, Oskar used his many contacts in Poland to assist in the clandestine mission to provide a false pretext to the invasion. According to Emilie Schindler, Oskar played a pivotal role: "Oskar paid a Polish soldier to get a Polish army uniform. It was then sent to Germany as a pattern for manufacturing more Polish uniforms that spies of the Third Reich would wear."[57] Hitler completed the plan when he attacked Poland shortly thereafter on September 1, 1939. He was, in his own words, protecting the Fatherland from Polish invaders.

German soldiers marching through Warsaw after invasion of Poland, 1939.
United States Holocaust Memorial Museum, courtesy of National Archives
and Records Administration, College Park

Oskar was right there playing an important role in the Nazi conquest of Europe. He did have one significant difference of opinion with the Nazis, however. A childhood friend of his was interviewed after the war, and his remarks give great insight into Oskar Schindler's inner core:

He was a Sudetenland fascist and a member of the Henlein Party which was later absorbed into Greater Germany's Nazi Party. Schindler was a true believer in everything but one factor—that was the racial policy. He was a friend of many local Jews in Svitavy. Schindler was friendly with our family, particularly my father, the Rabbi. He would have talks with my father about sophisticated Yiddish literature in Poland and Czechoslovakia ... and the anecdotes of ancient Jewish traditions of the villages of Eastern Poland.[58]

Schindler considered Jews his friends and equals and no amount of Nazi propaganda could change that.

ADHD Spies

In his early days as a spy, Oskar demonstrated behaviors that I recognize in myself and have seen time and again in ADHD people I work with. He jumped right into espionage without a thought of the dire and deadly consequences. He put his own and his wife's life in danger, and almost ended up dead. Many ADHD people act impulsively, which can often exact life-altering, or even life-ending, consequences. ADHD brains are not often good with boring and repetitive tasks but can be exceedingly useful when risk-taking fearlessness is required. This skill is indispensable for spies. Some people call this courage, which Oskar had plenty of.

When he started back with the Abwehr after being released from prison, Oskar had had time to reflect and learn some lessons. Generally, ADHDers are not all that adept at changing behavior, but Oskar had three months of isolation, which he seems to have used wisely. Whereas his initial time with the intelligence service suggested an impulsive and perhaps even inept nature, Oskar, a hands-on learner, rose quickly to become a reliable agent, whom the German high command entrusted with highly classified information and tasked with carrying out sensitive missions.[59] Those who knew him best talk about an intensity in Oskar during this time period, a high level of excitement and activity that brought out the best in him. The year before he arrived in Kraków, Poland—roughly October 1938 to September 1939—represented a new stage in his development, one in which negative traits and liabilities became important personal and professional assets.

Going back to his teenage years, Oskar had been known as a great liar. He could effortlessly spin a tale and make up lies on the spot without a second thought. Many ADHD people, like Oskar, are great, if not pathological, liars. Something about being swept to the margins of school and society sets one up to lie. When you've had the teacher's finger pointed at you repeatedly, it becomes preferable to lie rather than have to bear an adult's scorn over and over. Oskar the spy used fake names—Ing. Zeiler, Ost, Otto, and Schäfer—and collaborated with his colleagues to pull off elaborate deceptions. His greatest feat was that he pretended, as much as he could, to be a loyal subject to the Führer until the end of the war, a performance that was crucial to the more than one thousand people whose lives he saved. Good spies, like so many ADHD people, are often great liars.

Spies also must to be willing to break the law and have flexible scruples. Highly fixed ideas of right and wrong can get in the way of successful espionage. His numerous brushes with the law showed that this requirement of spying would not be a problem. During his tenure with the Abwehr, Oskar was involved in blackmail, sabotage, bribery, creating fake border incidents, destabilizing governments, and conquering non-aggressive nations. His skill at skirting laws and staying under the radar of enemy agents would eventually come into the service of saving Jewish people from the gas chamber. Time and again, he was confronted with overwhelming crises that he tackled with innovation and creativity. When scientists examine creative people, incidentally, they find that a high percentage also show significant ADHD symptomology.[60] Oskar, like all successful spies, had dirty hands, but without them, he never would have been able to brave the corrupt and brutal bureaucracy of Nazidom.

I am not saying, incidentally, that all ADHD people are would-be criminals, but most of us are drawn to intensity. Combine that with innate impulsivity and you have a potential recipe for disaster. I have been lucky that I have always found intensity without getting into legal troubles. When I was in high school, for example, I tutored the two granddaughters of a drug dealer. I went to her "drug house" three days a week in an unsavory Detroit neighborhood, where I was escorted into a basement bunker by an armed underling of the "queen of crack." Her street name was Petunia, but she was no fragile flower. In the late 1980s, she paid me twenty dollars an hour to work with her granddaughters. That was a lot of money for a sixteen-year-old student back then. I was nervous, but it was exciting. I also had bragging rights to my friends. Like most ADHD people, I am drawn to intensity and get depressed when I do not have it. Oskar was no different.

True to his ADHD nature, Oskar was also an extraordinarily social and talkative person. In school, he got in trouble for talking out of turn, and later on got in fights for not knowing when to keep his mouth shut. He loved going to parties and held some of Kraków's most memorable social events during the war years. Contact with people was a sustaining force in Oskar's life, energizing him and providing the fuel for his success. A prolific networker, Oskar had friends in virtually every level of the Nazi bureaucracy, from low-level clerks and secretaries all the way up to generals and admirals in the high command. He not only helped his Jewish workers, but he made connections with international Jewish aid groups, travelling regularly to Hungary and Turkey to meet with them. Although nowadays, antisocial individuals can engage in espionage through a computer or in cyberspace, spies generally have to be gifted social mixers. Oskar was a consummate "people person" who used that skill to recruit operatives, pull information out of contacts, and stay on the "right" side of the Nazis for the duration of the war. His greatest act of espionage was, incidentally, that he tricked the Nazis into believing he was just like them, which allowed him to ultimately save lives.

With the right mix of support and intensity, Oskar was an absolutely gifted man. He possessed a race-car brain that without the "right race" had crashed numerous times throughout the 1930s.[61] He thrived with intensity but had nothing positive to focus on, so he ended up creating powerful negative experiences that almost led to his execution. The war, however, brought him the extreme stimulation he craved and was neurologically built for. His wealth of talent finally began to flourish. He would need all of his gifts to deal with the incredibly dense evil that began to confront him on a daily basis.

Raising Schindler

☐ Oskar did not understand how his brain worked. You must compassionately inform your loved one about the inner workings of his or her brain and the consequent necessity of experimenting with different methods to help him or her function optimally. The "sit down, shut up" method probably will not work at home or school. *You* will first need to go to school on the brain. You will find a reading list at the end of this book for you to do just that, in addition to sections throughout. You then must teach your ADHD loved the lessons about the brain you have learned. I had one mother who put up full-color printouts of brain scans, showing the underactive brain patterns ADHD people experience with boring, routine, and low-intensity activities, as well as the fully active brain when interesting and exciting stimuli are being experienced. She took a cerebral and scientific matter and made it visual and easy to understand. She also took these printouts into school meetings to share with teachers and administrators. When you're dealing with a creative person, you will usually have to get creative yourself to help that individual understand his or her brain and place in the world.

☐ Without compassionate and informed dialogue, your loved one will likely experience some of Oskar's pitfalls. Your loved one is different, and that is wonderful as long as you can help him or her understand the nature of the differences and take appropriate actions. If we do not find positive ways of getting intensity and excitement in our lives, for example, we will, like Oskar, settle for negative intensity like gambling, substance use, starting arguments, and even breaking the law. For people like Oskar, intensity is not a frill, but rather a need that must be met.

☐ Substance use and abuse can be viewed as self-medication. If your loved one continues to struggle with maintaining prolonged attention and controlling impulsivity, medication is an option to be discussed with your healthcare provider. Oskar clearly self-medicated, but luckily, your loved one lives in an age of effective pharmacological treatments. This book, incidentally, is not a substitute for professional help!

☐ Your loved one may only thrive when he or she has an adventure or a passion. You must, at all costs, help him or her find it! This endeavor generally involves experimentation. In addition to the suggestions in Chapter 1, building rockets and robots, standup-comedy classes, martial arts training, and creative art classes are great places to start. Keep experimenting and you will find something that works.

☐ When your loved one has ADHD, or really any significant learning difference, you must work on yourself. You must find a way not only to inform your brain, but to temper your reactions. Negative reactions toward a person with ADHD will, over time, damage our self-esteem and self-efficacy. Mindfulness practices, meditation, yoga, and frequent discussions with a supportive network of friends and family can help you in this pursuit.

NOTES

1 All accounts point to a very contentious relationship with Oskar and his father. Oskar's father consistently expressed disapproval toward his son. I have taken details provided by Emilie and Oskar and forged them into a series of dialogues. Much of what we know about Hans Schindler comes from Emilie's accounts.

2 Oskar did realize he was different and told this in various ways to those close to him.

3 Schindler, E. & Rosenberg, E. (1996). *Where Light and Shadow Meet* (Trans. D. Koch). New York: W.W. Norton and Company, 27.

4 Schindler, E., 26.

5 Hall C., & Webster R. (2002). Traumatic symptomatology characteristics of adult children of alcoholics. *Journal of Drug Education* 32(3): 195–211; Hall C., & Webster R, & Powell E. (2003). Personal alcohol use in adult children of alcoholics. *Alcohol Research*, 8(4): 157–162.

6 Woititz, J. G. (1983). *Adult children of alcoholics*. Hollywood, FL: Heath Communications, Inc.

7 Bau, C., Almeida, S., Costa, F., Garcia, C., Elis, E., Onso, A., Spode, A., & Hutz, M. (2001). DRD4 and DAT1 as modifying genes in alcoholism: interaction with novelty seeking on level of alcohol consumption. *Molecular Psychiatry*, Vol. 6, Issue 1.

8 Beauchaine, T., Hinshaw, S., & Pang, K. (2010). Comorbidity of Attention-Deficit/Hyperactivity Disorder and Early-Onset Conduct Disorder: Biological, Environmental, and Developmental Mechanisms. *Clinical Psychology: Science & Practice*, Vol. 17 Issue 4; Barkley, R. (2006). *Attention Deficit-Hyperactivity Disorder*. New York: Guilford Press.

9 Emilie has talked often about town perceptions about her husband. These anecdotes can be found extensively in Schindler, E. & Rosenberg, E. (1996). *Where Light and Shadow Meet* (Trans. D. Koch). New York: W.W. Norton and Company.

10 O'Neil.

11 There was conflict in the Schindler household and like any good parent in this situation, Oskar's mother feared her son would repeat the sins of the father. This exchange between mother and son is my creation, going off of sources that briefly touch on the relation between them, as well as an understanding of the fact that she did not drink, and disapproved of this behavior in her son and husband. Emilie

describes Oskar's mother as kind, patient, and elegant. She and Oskar were quite close.

12 Oskar definitely aspired, like most sons, to achieve a higher status than his father. Hand Schindler clearly did not have the mental balance and maturity to bless and honor his son's abilities, so, like many sons, Oskar spent a lifetime seeking, largely unconsciously, his father's approval.

13 We do not find any record of Schindler's conversations from his mother, but much can be inferred from remarks Emilie has made concerning this relationship.

14 O'Neil.

15 Ibid.

16 Ibid.

17 *Schindler's List.* Dir. Steven Spielberg. 1993. Universal Pictures. DVD.

18 From Emilie's book and other accounts (O'Neil, Crowe), it is clear that Oskar squandered this money and this caused marital conflict.

19 Schindler, E. & Rosenberg, E. (1996). *Where Light and Shadow Meet* (Trans. D. Koch). New York: W.W. Norton and Company, 27.

20 Breyer, J., Botzet, A., Winters, K., Stinchfield, R., August, G., & Realmuto, G. (2009). Young adult gambling behaviors and their relationship with the persistence of ADHD. *Journal of Gambling Studies*, Vol. 25, Issue 2.

21 Rodriguez-Jimenez, R., Avila, C., Jimenez-Arriero, M., Ponce, G., Monasor, R., Jimenez, M., Aragües, M., Hoenicka, J., Rubio, G., & Palomo, T. (2006). Impulsivity and sustained attention in pathological gamblers: influence of childhood ADHD history. *Journal of Gambling Studies*, Vol. 22, Issue 4.

22 Lawrence, A., Luty, J., Bogdan, N., Sahakian, B., & Clark, L. (2009). Impulsivity and response inhibition in alcohol dependence and problem gambling, *Psychopharmacology*, Vol. 207, Issue 1.

23 Dang, L., Samanez-Larkin, G., Young, J., Cowan, R., Kessler, R., and Zald, D. (2014). Caudate asymmetry is related to attentional impulsivity and an objective measure of ADHD-like attentional problems in healthy adults. *Brain Structure and Function*.

24 Brown, T. (2014). *Smart but Stuck*. San Francisco: Jossey Bass.

25 O'Neil.

26 Ibid.

27 O'Neil, 40.

28 Hallowell, E. & Ratey, J. (2003). *Driven to Distraction*. Simon and Schuster: New York.

29 Nigg, J. (2006). What Causes ADHD?: Understanding What Goes Wrong and Why. New York: Guilford Press; Barkley, R. (2006). Attention Deficit Hyperactivity Disorder: A Handbook for Diagnosis and Treatment. New York: Guilford Press.

30 Ibid.

31 Rosenberg, M., Finn, E., Scheinost, D., Xenophon, P., Xilin, S., Constable, R.T., and Chun, M. (2015). A Neuromarker of sustained attention from whole brain functional connectivity, Nature Neuroscience. Online. Available at http://www.nature.com/articles.

32 Oskar was forever on the hunt for some new adventure and had an unremitting restlessness until the day he died. This dialogue is one I largely crafted, based on source material.

33 Emilie counseled patience and persistence, but she seems to have made little impact on Oskar in these areas.

34 The historical record indicates a constant anxiety in Emilie, which can be easily appreciated when one considers Oskar's impulsive nature.

35 Schindler, E., p. 28.

36 Shirer, W. (1960). The Rise and Fall of the Third Reich. Simon and Schuster: New York, 359.

37 Kuras, B. The Sudenten German Lie and the Survival Instinct, Czechoslovak Society of Arts and Sciences. Online. Available at http://www.svu2000.org/issues/kuras7.htm.

38 Smelser, R. (1975). The Sudeten Problem: 1933-1938. Middletown, CT: Wesleyan University Press.

39 Shirer.

40 O'Neil.

41 The record is clear that she influenced Oskar's interest in working for the Nazis.

42 Schindler, E.

43 O'Neil.

44 Ibid.

45 Hitler, A. (1923). Mein Kampf, p. 469. Online. Available at http://www.angelfire.com/folk/bigbaldbob88/MeinKampf.pdf.

46 Schindler, E., 31.

47 The Sudeten Germans overwhelming cheered for and supported this development.

48 See Schindler, E. for more on Emilie's takes on both Hitler and Henlein.

49 Oskar had an ongoing habit of dismissing Emilie's fears and concerns, although many of these would have seemed completely reasonable to a person with a logical mind.

50 This exchange takes literary license, based on Oskar's account and the historical record. We do know that Major Von Korab was one of his main contacts initially.

51 Oskar made very little effort to cover up what he was doing.

52 This name is my creation.

53 We know the types of questions Oskar asked from the court transcripts that survive as well as eyewitness corroboration. These exchanges and characters here are of my creation, seeking to forge a bit more narrative from the dry facts. Leo Pruscha was a railway worker and friend of Oskar Schindler who was also arrested as part of Czechoslovak police investigations.

54 O'Neil, Crowe.

55 This dialogue is to some extent my creation. Schindler, like many Sudeten Germans, was whipped into frenzy. Germany must have seemed all powerful and unstoppable. Hitler had, after all, freed him from jail and execution. And yes, he proved that he was willing to die for the Third Reich, a fact that helped account for his immense standing in Nazi circles of power.

56 Shirer.

57 Schindler, E. O'Neil.

58 O'Neil, 59.

59 O'Neil.

60 Healey, D., & Rucklidge, J. (2008). The Relationship between ADHD and Creativity, *ADHD Report*, Vol.16, No. 3.

61 Again, this metaphor was coined by Ned Hallowell.

Chapter 3 Friends, Enemies, and Protectors

I'm not a saint by any means.
I'm a self-indulgent person with more faults than the average man.

—Oskar Schindler

Battling the Forces of Darkness

SOMETIMES WE FIND OUR passion, but often passion finds us. "If I ever get out of here," Oskar Schindler told himself as he languished in prison awaiting execution, "I will do something extraordinary."[1] To fulfill that promise to himself, he battled forces so dark that the name of their leader, Adolph Hitler, is now synonymous with Satan. Oskar had one foot in the world of Nazi terror and the other in the field of human decency. This seemingly untenable dichotomy prompted his wife, Emilie, to title the book about her experiences, *Where Light and Shadow Meet*.

"Oskar is changing,"[2] Emilie told her friend, Bertha Hoffman.[3] "Maybe changing is the wrong word. It is like a part of him that has been there the whole time, patiently waiting, has finally come out. He is fully present like he has never been before, but I worry about these Nazis. He is not like them, but

Oskar is so impressionable that I worry their evil will prevail over him."[4]

Oskar Schindler was a member of the Nazi party. In fact, he proudly wore Nazi party emblems on his clothes and had been an early and enthusiastic supporter of Hitler. What's more, he spied for the "Fatherland" and had been sentenced to death for his service to the greater German Reich. The Nazis viewed Oskar Schindler as a great German patriot. To attempt to understand his monumental deeds, one must learn some basics about the Nazis and how Oskar used their prejudice and greed to defeat them.

For Oskar, the appeal of Nazism lay in its glorification of Germany, which held the promise of increasing his status and wealth along with that of his fellow Sudeten Germans in Czechoslovakia. "We have been held back in this country," Oskar told his friends. "Hitler and Henlein are just trying to level the playing field. I believe they have our best interests at heart."[5] While seeing logic in tying his fortunes to those of Nazi Germany, Oskar did not believe one of the deep and defining philosophical tenets of the Nazis, that most of the world's problems could be traced to the Jewish people. He assured Emilie that his support of Hitler had nothing to do with anti-Semitism, but was simply a function of his desire to help himself and his fellow Czechoslovak Germans: "Emilie, I have had Jewish friends since I was a small boy. I have no problem with Jewish people, and I rather like Jewish culture. The Nazis will never change that."[6]

Emilie's apprehensions are easy to appreciate. The German government unabashedly proclaimed its anti-Semitism to the world. One of the most insidious aspects of the Nazis' philosophical system is that they were so convinced—brainwashed—that the Jews were a scourge against the human race that the Nazis actually presumed they were helping

Schindler with Nazi officers at a dinner party in Kraków, 1942. *United States Holocaust Memorial Museum, courtesy of Leopold Page Photographic Collection*

humanity by getting rid of the Jews. "The world may hate us now," Reinhard Heydrich told his wife, "but one day they will all thank us for getting rid of the Jews."[7] The Nazi belief in the biological superiority of pure Germans—the Aryans—rose to the level of religious fervor. They believed that a group of no-madic people from thousands of years ago, the Aryans, had been a superior race responsible for all great civilizations, like ancient Greece and Rome. Their superior traits had largely been lost, the Nazis believed, except in the German people. "It is our moral duty to subjugate and destroy the world's 'inferi-or' peoples," Heinrich Himmler proclaimed to a group of Nazi recruits. "Jews, Gypsies, Slavs, and homosexuals, they simply take up space. We are the descendants of the Aryans and we owe it to the world to not only claim our unique place in his-tory, but also to protect and purify our superior traits."[8,9] The Nazis couched their commitment to this *cause* in a perverse understanding of Charles Darwin's idea of "natural selection," and its corollary, "survival of the fittest."

Ethnic Germans like Oskar Schindler were receptive to this message. "Pure Germans, Aryans," the Sudeten German leaders repeatedly insisted, "are biologically best-suited to rule the world, and have an obligation to stamp out racial impurity and imperfection."[10] Just as great white sharks possessed biological advantages—size, powerful jaws, sensory adaptations—that allowed them to rule over the sea, the Aryans were biologically superior, the Nazis declared, and thus were destined to rule the world. This mindset has come to be known as Social Darwinism, the incorrect application of Darwin's evolutionary principles to human social groupings. External differences, like hair, eye, and skin color, do not correlate with higher or lower intelligence, or impart unique gifts as the Nazis believed. Different tones of skin are simply ... skin deep.

Oskar's Psychotic Friends

Relying on flawed notions of race instead of science, the Nazis presumed blue eyes and blond hair to be the external manifestations of Aryan superiority. They thought they could, with restrictive marriage laws and racial purity standards, increase superior Aryan qualities and eliminate inferior human traits. To this end, they examined the German population and decided to take action by isolating and then exterminating mentally and physically challenged Germans as part of a secret initiative called T-4. They killed thousands of people under this program; many of those who administered T-4 would go on to staff and direct the death camps that killed millions more. Oskar Schindler acquainted himself with many of these murderous SS men and their henchmen.

Oskar regularly partied, for example, with Julian Scherner, the top SS officer in the Kraków area who was responsible for signing off on the deportation and execution of tens of thousands of people. Schindler not only drank with him, but also paid him over sixty thousand dollars in bribes during the war.[11]

"Everybody seems to know you," Julian Scherner told him at one of the many parties Oskar hosted at his lavish Kraków apartment. "How is it that you have so many friends in high places?"[12] Oskar always answered such questions evasively. "One hopes to have many friends in life, Julian, and I do think I have been blessed in that way."

Scherner's boss, Heinrich Himmler, was the high priest of the murderous and destructive Nazi belief system. He ruled over the SS, the elite military organization within the Nazi Party that contained the most fanatical and committed members. SS, incidentally, stands for *Schutzstaffel*, which means body, or protection, corps; the organization started by providing security at Nazi party rallies and functions. Himmler, who prior to his involvement with Nazism had been a chicken farmer, had deliberately based the design of the SS on the Jesuits, a highly disciplined and trained order of Catholic priests. Himmler is said to have admired the order's obedience and organization, while Schindler despised the SS for its evil religiosity. Himmler wanted men who could be trained to exhibit ruthlessness as well as to unquestioningly follow orders. Only the most "Aryan-looking" Germans were allowed to join the elite order, which meant relatively tall, preferably blond-haired and blue-eyed, as well as athletically competent. Schindler came to hold the SS in contempt, referring to them as "those fanatics."

While Schindler counted Jews among his good friends, Himmler and his top lieutenant, Heydrich, zealously believed that most of Germany's, and the world's, problems could be attributed to the Jewish people, who were like a poison that carried the destructive capacity to pollute the Aryan German blood. While this assertion may seem outlandish, the men who controlled the German government from 1933-1945 considered it the solid and reasonable basis for public policy. Heydrich, whose Nazi intelligence-gathering organization put him in direct conflict with Oskar Schindler, said that the

Himmler reviewing a unit of SS troops during the war. *United States Holocaust Memorial Museum, courtesy of James Blevins*

Jewish people were a contagion, a source of societal sickness that had caused Germany to lose wars, average Germans to lose jobs, and the whole nation to lose its power and prestige in the world. All of Germany's major problems, Heydrich and the Nazis fervently maintained, could be traced back to the Jews.

Discussions at the highest levels of the German government sought a solution to this perceived problem, which only increased in complexity after Germany took over Poland in September 1939 because this move added millions of Jews to the Reich. "How do you propose we solve this Jewish problem?"[13] Himmler asked on an extremely cold December morning in Berlin in 1939. Himmler, Heydrich, and Alfred Rosenberg, a Nazi "intellectual," had gathered for breakfast to discuss what they considered Germany's most pressing challenge. "Europe is to be combed from East to West for Jews," Heydrich replied. "We will separate them, isolate them, and then once we have them centralized we can figure out a final solution." Rosenberg added, "Germany will regard the Jewish question as solved only after the very last Jew has left the greater German living space. Europe will have its Jewish question solved only after the very last Jew has left the continent."[14]

A Steady Diet of Terror

When Hitler came to power in 1933, Heydrich was largely in charge of arresting political opponents of the regime and was "the implementer," the one who put anti-Jewish ideals into practical policies of persecution.[15] Jews were progressively prohibited from ever-widening spheres of German life. This happened slowly, in stages, and the rest of the world was so absorbed in the economic tragedy of the Great Depression that Nazi persecution of the Jews went somewhat unnoticed and largely unchallenged. Oskar did not immediately comprehend the full horrors of Nazi anti-Semitism, a point highlighted by his utter shock at the treatment of the Jews when he arrived in Kraków, Poland. "I did not believe the reports that came out of Germany,"[16] Oskar wrote to Emilie shortly after he went to Kraków. "It is much worse than I could ever have imagined. They not only beat the Jews, but they mistreat the Poles, as well. I am not like them, Emilie."[17]

German soldiers occupying Poland in 1939, on the other hand, had witnessed six years of increasingly brutal anti-Semitism in Germany. Many of the German soldiers had, at the very least, become desensitized to the daily and almost routine violence directed at Jews. They had seen the situation gradually deteriorate. At first, Jewish stores in Germany were boycotted. Jews were slowly but methodically expelled from jobs in the government. Jewish doctors were forbidden to treat "Aryans."

Jews outside a shop that had its windows broken by German invaders, 1941.
United States Holocaust Memorial Museum, courtesy of Rafael Scharf

They were limited as to how much money they could keep, and then forced to wear a Star-of-David armband in public, making it easier for the Nazis to identify them in order to exclude them from public life and to humiliate them in the streets. Anti-Semitism was a fact of life, and ordinary German soldiers had received a steady diet of propaganda in school, social clubs, the movies and radio, and even from loud speakers that broadcast in the streets. Large numbers of Sudeten Germans certainly held anti-Semitic beliefs, and the Sudeten German newspapers regularly featured anti-Semitic articles, but Oskar was not fully exposed to the barbaric treatment of the Jews until he went to Poland.

"Hitler has brainwashed the German people,"[18] Oskar wrote to Emilie. "I see that the reports that had been coming out of Germany were, if anything, underplaying the brutality."[19] So successful was the brainwashing effort in Germany prior to the start of World War II that on the night when the

Nazis burned and destroyed Jewish buildings across the country, passersby simply watched. No one tried to put out the fires. This night, known as *Kristallnacht*, the night of broken glass, occurred in November 1938. Heydrich, who Schindler quickly grew to hate, was one of the chief organizers of this terror. Bands of Nazi thugs under Heydrich's direction roamed the streets on this day, breaking the glass of Jewish shops, beating Jews, and burning down 267 synagogues throughout Germany. Tens of thousands of Jews were arrested and sent to lives of extreme deprivation and torture in concentration camps, where many died. Herman Göring, essentially Hitler's second in command, even made the Jews pay for the damage and cleanup, imposing on Germany's Jews a fine of almost half a billion dollars. Appropriating Jewish property quickened its pace after *Kristallnacht*, a practice from which Oskar Schindler would actually enjoy great benefits. Germany's Jews had lost all of their rights by this time. Soon after, most of these people would lose their homes, too, as they were "resettled." *Resettlement* was code for forcing Jews to leave their homes and then cramming them into ghettoes, mostly in Poland. Ghettoes were small, densely packed parts of cities in which six, seven, eight people or more were crammed into one small room. There they suffered greatly from malnutrition, starvation, lice, and disease. Ultimately, millions of these folks were transported to death camps, including Auschwitz, Belżec, and Treblinka. Oskar Schindler, a man with numerous high-level Nazi contacts, learned early on of the purpose of these camps, a fact that fueled his desire to save his Jewish workers.

German vs German

Oskar Schindler can be counted among the truly courageous Germans. He was a rare rebel in a German system that had taken enormous care to weed out any opposition. By the time of *Kristallnacht*, Germany had become a virtual terror state.

Anyone who said one unkind or unsupportive word about the Nazis could be summarily sent to one of the dreaded concentrations camps. Heydrich played a huge role in this machinery of terror. At the very outset of the Nazi rise to power, Heydrich determined to create a system of domestic spies that could easily weed out anyone who made even the most innocent criticism of the Nazi regime. He recruited two hundred thousand ordinary Germans as "block wardens" who spied on their fellow citizens.[20] "German will turn in German,"[21] Heydrich said. "The German people will do most of our work for us."[22] It was not uncommon for German children to report their own parents to the police; friends turned in friends, and neighbors turned in neighbors. The Nazis invaded the very fabric and fiber of Germany society. One word against the Nazis, even in the safety of one's home, could land an ordinary German in one of the growing number of horrific concentration camps such as Dachau, Ravensbruck, Buchenwald, and Sachsenhausen, where treatment included daily beatings, starvation rations, and the complete stripping away of an individual's humanity. These tactics were later exported to the work and death camps in Poland.

In addition to being one of Himmler's top lieutenants in the SS, Heydrich had also set up what is known as the Sicherheitsdienst (SD), the Nazi security service responsible for domestic spying and intelligence gathering. This position put him increasingly in conflict with a high-ranking friend of Oskar Schindler, Admiral Wilhelm Canaris, head of Germany's army intelligence unit, the Abwehr. "I am glad I work for Canaris and not that animal, Heydrich,"[23] Oskar told Emilie. "He is not a real German in my book. Real Germans are hard-working, kind, and helpful. Heydrich is a beast."

As Germany gained new lands and territories, that beast sought to increase the scope of the SD. This desire caused grave conflict with Admiral Canaris, a conflict in which

Oskar Schindler was inextricably embroiled. In fact, in 1940, Schindler traveled to Turkey with orders from Canaris to clean up an intelligence mess, as skirmishes heated up between Canaris's Abwehr and Heydrich's SD. "Emilie, I have come to realize that I am at my best when I have something to fight against," Oskar said. "I love Germany, but I hate those thugs in the SD, SS, and Gestapo. They give good Germans a bad name. I intend to do something about that."[24]

As he went to Turkey, Oskar entered a very bad situation that was brewing all across German-held territory. Canaris had dispatched Schindler to see if he could broker a deal to end the growing rivalry between the two German spy agencies in Turkey. He was not successful, but Schindler was so well connected that he spent time during his stay with many German dignitaries, including Ambassador Franz von Papen. "I am unimpressed by Von Papen," Schindler recounted to Emilie. "He is no true believer in Nazism, but he is an ineffective leader."[25] Oskar nevertheless reveled at being treated to such high-level meetings in such luxurious surroundings as the German embassy in Turkey. Such encounters enhanced his prestige within the German Reich, helping in later years to keep him from falling into the hands of Nazi zealots who would come to hate him and who would have preferred he spent the war in a concentration camp.

Oskar's rising star only brightened after this trip, in spite of the fact that the troubles in Turkey worsened. The battle there can be seen on the surface as simply a turf war between the SD and the Abwehr. On a deeper level, however, the Turkish turmoil was rooted in a growing conflict within the German Reich. On the one side stood the extreme anti-Semites. On the other were high-ranking German officers and politicians who did not share the genocidal fervor of the Nazis, but were nonetheless German patriots. Oskar Schindler was a member of the latter camp, a point highlighted by the fact that his spying activities were done exclusively for Canaris's Abwehr, not Heydrich's SD.

Oskar loved being a spy. "I feel fully alive," he told friends. "This is the work I was born to do. I have faults, more than the average person, but it seems that my faults are allowing me to charm these Nazis. I know how their minds work, and that allows me to outwit them."[26] Oskar was a deviant in many ways, but these traits, as he said, gave him much in common with the Nazi thugs he encountered in Poland. A youth who has been rejected from the school system, as Oskar had been, and who finds himself with demeaning labels such as "Schindler the Swindler," is at particularly high risk for aberrant behavior and for finding other underachieving and perhaps antisocial young people. Examining the leaders of the extermination program in Germany leads one to the conclusion that while they certainly did not all have ADHD, by and large, they were all underachievers, individuals who had not succeeded to their potential. Remember, Himmler had been a country chicken farmer before heading the Nazi terror apparatus. Heydrich had been thrown out of the German navy in disgrace, and Hitler had been rejected from art school. Underachieving people populated the highest levels of the Nazi state. Oskar had an affinity for these types of people, which helps account for his ability to forge friendships with them. Scientific data suggest that having been peer rejected and lacking success for many years seem to predispose ADHD young people to pick deviant friends,[27] a fact that further increases the risks for substance abuse, criminal behavior, and a host of psychological and social difficulties. Oskar certainly did have these issues, but some goodness deep within him kept him psychologically far enough away from the forces of evil that he was able to help others.

Heydrich and Himmler, unlike Oskar, showed no signs of executive function deficits, which are among the hallmarks of ADHD. Nevertheless, a case could easily be made that both men, like Oskar and ADHD adolescents, had a marked tendency to associate with deviants. After all, Heydrich and Himmler exhibited aberrant behavior that will be remembered as long as humankind remains on this earth. However, their deviance was not constrained by the difficulties and challenges of ADHD. Their ability to plan, organize, manage their time, execute actions, and allow their behavior to be governed by the promise of future reward, and not the impulses of the moment, was incredible. These men had such a high level of executive functioning, in fact, that they can be personally "credited" with millions of deaths. Without these two men, the Holocaust still would have likely happened, but their efficiency of action and planning helped ensure that the Nazi machinery of death worked with impeccable precision. They made detailed calculations, set up extensive systems of organization and training, and executed their plans with flawless follow through.

Heydrich and Himmler, and their Nazi compatriots, were zealots, people so convinced of the moral correctness of their philosophical system that they stopped questioning their beliefs. They were so persuaded of the accuracy of their worldview that they considered implementing it a sacred duty. Oskar and most ADHDers, on the other hand, are as far from zealots as one can get. In fact, ADHD people are often rebels. They are the ones who find delight in opposition, in breaking the rules and beating the system. In Oskar's case, this tendency was to the great fortune of approximately twelve hundred Jewish people and thousands of their descendants.

Oskar had a different brain, one which made certain aspects of life difficult. His life experiences, however, gave him tremendous empathy for people in need, as well as an almost instinctual resistance to authority. These two features made him a very formidable foe.

ADHD: It's in the brain

Many uninformed individuals still persist in the notion that ADHD results from poor parenting, laziness, or a character flaw in the individual. Oskar certainly had clinical dysfunction in his family, and it would be enticing to link his ADHD traits to flaws in his upbringing. Brain research continues to clarify, however, that certain regions of the brain function atypically in ADHD individuals. The prefrontal cortex, the basal ganglia, and the parietal regions, for example, show significant impairment in activation patterns for ADHD individuals. These regions are associated with the executive functions impaired in ADHD: working memory, the ability to plan, organize, and manage time. When children without a history of executive function deficits experience traumatic brain injury that damages one or more of these regions, these deficits often emerge. An even more stunning example of the ADHD-brain connection can be found by examining the

The Other Germany

Oskar's brain accounts for his extreme trouble following through and staying on task. His friend, Admiral Wilhelm Canaris, was the opposite. Never having fallen fully under Hitler's spell, he, like Oskar, played a dangerously deceptive game with the Führer (this word simply means, "leader"). The admiral was not an underachiever. He had been awarded numerous commendations, including the elite military decoration, The Iron Cross, which was given to those who had served with distinction and bravery in World War I. He continued serving in the navy after the war. Canaris was, upon Hitler's ability to delay an impulse, which is impaired in ADHD, and is, in fact, a diagnostic criterion. The caudate nucleus of the brain, which has already been discussed, is one of the brain areas strongly associated with the ability to control impulses. Children with no history of impulsivity who experience damage to this part of the brain often become impulsive. Brain scans of ADHD boys show a tendency for irregularly shaped caudate nuclei as well as an asymmetry between the right and left sides.[28] Further, brain scans show irregular brain-wave patterns in ADHD people, as well as underactivity in key brain regions. Again, ADHD is condition with strong correlation to atypical and irregularly functioning brains, structural anomalies, and cerebral pattern differences. The evidence is overwhelming, by virtue of the executive function deficits he so strongly exhibited, that Oskar had an atypically-functioning brain.

rise to power, promoted as head of German military intelligence because at that point he had amassed a great deal of intelligence-gathering experience and was highly regarded by his military and political colleagues.

"I like you, Canaris,"[29] Hitler said to the admiral when they discussed his recent promotion. "You see clearly the dangers of that horde of Communist Slavs. They are sub-humans and need to be wiped out, or at the very least, enslaved to serve the German people. I need you to help me defeat them." The two men had found common ground in their mutual hatred for Communism and the Soviet Union. Hitler linked Communism to what he saw as a worldwide Jewish conspiracy.

He saw Communists as a destabilizing and corruptive force in Germany. In fact, when Hitler and his henchmen burned the Reichstag in 1933 to create an atmosphere of emergency, they blamed this incident on the Communists. In spite of Canaris and Hitler agreeing on their mutual disdain for Communism, however, the two began to have serious disagreements as early as 1938, when the admiral tried in vain to talk Hitler out of his plans to absorb Oskar Schindler's homeland, the Sudetenland of Czechoslovakia. "*Mein Führer,* I fear that the great powers of the world—the United States, France, Great Britain, and the Soviet Union—will rise up and unite if we embark on the course you have chosen."[30] Hitler glibly replied, "Nonsense. I will drive a wedge between them. They have no stomach for war, and that will be their undoing."[31] While Hitler saw logic in his reasoning, Canaris thought his plans extremely reckless.

Canaris was a man of action, and he became entwined with a group of high-ranking German military officers and powerbrokers who eventually saw Hitler as a threat to Germany's long-term prosperity. There is strong evidence to suggest that during this period, Canaris began playing a double game by increasing contacts with British intelligence, Germany's enemy.[32] Some scholars believe he even warned the British about Hitler's plans to attack Czechoslovakia and Poland, and numerous evidence exists to conclusively show that Canaris maintained contacts with British intelligence throughout World War II, hoping to keep channels open so a peace could eventually be negotiated once Hitler was out of the way.[33] Canaris's organization had followed Hitler's orders, however, and had begun espionage activities in Czechoslovakia the summer before the takeover of the Sudetenland, employing numerous spies, including Oskar Schindler.

Discussions inside the Abwehr, in which Oskar Schindler certainly participated, involved growing concern about the treatment of the Jews and the Poles. Soon after the invasion of Poland, Canaris himself took these concerns all the way up to the supreme commander of German armed forces, General Keitel. Keitel, incidentally, was tried and executed after the war. Most of his crimes related to his approval of the rounding up and execution of political prisoners in occupied territories. Like many German war criminals, he claimed to have been simply following orders. An excerpt from Canaris's own diary relates to a conversation he had with Keitel early in the war:

> I told Keitel I was aware of extensive executions planned in Poland and that the nobility and clergy were to be particularly exterminated. The Wehrmacht [German army] would, in the final reckoning, be held responsible for these atrocities carried out under their very noses.[34]

Canaris saw his country going down a dark path, but for the most part, those in power were not worried.

By 1941, Canaris was thoroughly convinced that Hitler had wandered astray. The admiral filed numerous complaints that Germany had been in gross violation of the rules of war established by the Geneva Convention. The increasing brutality against civilians in German-occupied lands and the mistreatment and killing of the Jews convinced Canaris that Germany would be held responsible for war crimes after the war was over.[35] This concern grew after Hitler attacked the Soviet Union in June1941. At this time, the dreaded Einsatzgruppen, or death squads, followed behind the German army's advance, rounded up Jews in the Soviet Union, and brutally executed them. At places like Babi Yar in the Ukraine, hundreds of thousands of Jewish people were, over the course of several months, shot in the back of the head and buried in mass graves. Reinhard Heydrich was directly in charge of these murder squads. Admiral Canaris was outraged that soldiers in the Wehrmacht had been forced, under Heydrich's direct insistence, to assist in these mass shootings. He sent numerous statements of objection to the German high command. Keitel replied, "You are squeamish, weak, and ignorant of military affairs, Canaris. Leave the fighting to those with the stomach for war."[36] Himmler himself, however, was apparently quite squeamish. He vomited when he witnessed these executions during an inspection of the front line, an incident reported by his adjutant, Karl Wolff.[37] This experience convinced Himmler that a more methodical means needed to be found to carry out the mass murder of the Jews. Himmler called for the implementation of a "more humane" system; by humane, he meant a method that would be less psychologically damaging to German personnel, not less painful and horrific for the victims.

By the time Himmler was touring the front lines in the fall of 1941, Canaris had already fallen somewhat out of favor with German military leaders because of his opposition to Hitler's policy of aggression and conquest. He pleaded with the high command that attacking the Soviet Union would ultimately lead to Germany's downfall. In another reply to Canaris, General Keitel stated, "My dear Canaris, you may know your way about the field of intelligence, but you are a sailor. Don't try to give the army a lesson in military strategy."[38] With the initial success of the invasion of the Soviet Union, Canaris fell even more out of favor, a fact used unsuccessfully by his rival, Reinhard Heydrich, to strip the Abwehr of some of its power and influence. Canaris's opposition to war, brutality, and the extermination of the Jews meant that his activities did, however, come under increasing suspicion from Nazi true believers. As Canaris came under greater SS scrutiny, so did Oskar Schindler.

At this time, late 1941, both Schindler and Canaris amplified their anti-Nazi activities. Schindler began employing more Jews in his factory, giving them extra rations, and protecting them from the Nazi guards, as well as warning

Jews living in the ghetto of impending German "actions," or roundups. Canaris increasingly helped desperate individuals escape the clutches of the Nazis. From eyewitnesses and his later diary entries, it becomes apparent that Canaris was not only worried about a German defeat and that members of the armed forces would be held responsible for Nazi atrocities, but he also became progressively more distraught over the treatment of the Jews. He and Schindler had both been, in fact, branded by many high-ranking Nazis as "Jew lovers." Canaris, like Schindler, helped Jewish people in his hometown both hide from the Gestapo and get out of Germany. He also used his influence to get prison releases for German friends of his who had been sent to concentration camps for helping Jews.[39] Early in the war, Canaris helped prominent Polish and Jewish leaders escape the Third Reich. In many cases, he used his extensive diplomatic contacts in neutral Spain to offer safe passage to Jewish and political refugees.[40] He even helped facilitate the escape from Warsaw of a prominent Jewish leader, Rebbe Yosef Yitzchak Schneersohn.[41] Instead of letting the Nazis stamp out Judaism, Canaris helped the Jewish people survive, and some he helped, like Rebbe Schneersohn, established communities all around the world that helped European Jewry re-root itself after the Holocaust. Canaris filed several objections with the high command regarding the atrocities of the SS and the Gestapo, but he was rebuffed each and every time, and his protestations slowly eroded his credibility with Heydrich, Himmler, and Hitler. Canaris's behavior provided Oskar Schindler with a powerful example that he ultimately followed.

Oskar the Opportunist

Canaris tried to save his country, along with scores of innocent individuals who were targeted by the Nazis. For his efforts, the admiral ultimately paid with his life: The Nazis hung him with piano wire, much slower and more painful than "normal" hanging, just a few weeks before the war ended. His connection to Schindler played an enormous and pivotal role in Oskar's ability to save his Jewish workers. The fly-by-the-seat-of his-pants ADHDer had little use for rules and regulations, so he frequently found himself in trouble. A natural rebel, Schindler seemed to take delight in breaking the rules, a habit that went back to his school days. Without Canaris and other friends in high places, Oskar likely would have languished in prison, and maybe even been sent to a concentration camp. Wilhelm Koppe, an SS colonel and area police chief in Poland, told Schindler in 1943, "You insult my officers regularly and were it not for your service to the Fatherland, I would put you in a concentration camp this very instant. We know you are nothing but a Jew lover, Herr Schindler."[42]

Concentration camps did not scare Oskar. In fact, the Nazi concentration camp culture was one of Oskar's chief allies. While many people view the death camp, Auschwitz, for example, with understandable horror, for members of the SS, the death camp was a plum posting.[43] SS men and women stationed at the death camp regularly helped themselves to the personal valuables and effects left behind by their victims before they were murdered. When Jewish people were given orders to show up for "resettlement," they were generally allowed to take one bag. Into this piece of luggage they typically carried their most valuable items, hoping they could be used to purchase food and clothing and maybe even their very lives. SS soldiers considered Auschwitz a very desirable posting because they were far from the front lines of battle, and they enjoyed the booty they stole from the Jews who had had the misfortune of being sent to the camp.[44] This practice reached such epidemic proportions that the whole camp was investigated by the Gestapo, and many members of the SS were actually arrested, not, it should be pointed out, for their brutality to the Jews and others who made their way there, but for failing to send the belongings of these people back to Berlin.[45,46]

Schindler used this corruption to great effect. He bribed dozens of army and SS officials. He bribed guards in his factory to treat his workers humanely. Some bribes were as simple as a bottle of soda or a beer. For higher-ranking officials, monthly monetary payoffs were distributed on a fixed schedule. Bribery was the glue that held Schindler's ultimate plans together. While Himmler envisioned the SS as a group of individuals above suspicion and beyond reproach, many SS men, from guards up to generals, used their positions to personally profit. In the first place, their profits were won on the backs of the Jews, but in the second, whatever they stole represented items not given to the Nazi state. They stole from the Jews and many other occupied peoples, but they also stole from the very government to which they professed total allegiance.[47] Oskar used this hypocrisy to beat them at their own game.

Yes, Oskar did ultimately beat the Nazis, but he also played the game, which meant that he enriched himself at the expense of the Jews—and Poles—living in Kraków and those who were sent there. The Nazis invaded Poland on September 1, 1939, the official start date of World War II. The Germans took Kraków less than a week later, and the whole country capitulated a few weeks after that; Schindler arrived in the city soon after, and he was still taking orders from the Abwehr as a spy. "Set up a network of agents to open up businesses in Kraków," Oskar's orders from the Abwehr read. "Businesses will give them a plausible cover."[48] These agents, under the directive of Admiral Canaris, were meant to keep an eye not only on military targets, but also on the SS, the Gestapo, and Heydrich's SD.

In the weeks and months that followed the swift German victory in Poland, throngs of Germans flocked to the city, hoping to strike it rich. These fortune hunters, Oskar among them, came to Poland at a time of unimaginable carnage and chaos. The German army had taken over the country in less than three weeks, and as early as September 21, disturbing directives flowed from Berlin. First of all, large areas of western Poland were annexed directly to the German Reich. The other areas included much of central and southern Poland. Called the General Government, the Germans eventually incorporated parts of Ukraine into this zone. The Nazis, under the governor of this area, Hans Frank, meant to expel the Jews and enslave the Poles, and in some cases, make way for German "settlers." Heydrich's orders at this time centered on herding the Jews into cities in preparing for what he called the "Final Solution," a term that would later take on an ominous meaning. Heydrich also spoke in numerous communiqués about a general "housecleaning," getting rid of not only the Jews, but also the Polish leadership, such as politicians, soldiers, and teachers. In fact, thousands of Poles were swiftly arrested and executed in the first few months of Nazi occupation.[49] Many thousands more filled the jails, incarcerated indefinitely for offenses such as "rude remarks to a German." As the guide on my first tour of Auschwitz said, "Any reason was a good reason to punish people the Nazis saw as enemies." Incidentally, Auschwitz was opened as a prison camp in the spring of 1940, housing thousands of Polish "political" prisoners, most of whom died there. It was only later that the death camp was added to this operation. As Jews and Poles lost their rights, businesses, and property, Oskar and other opportunistic Germans profited handsomely.[50]

Amidst the theft of property and decimation of Polish and Jewish society, Jews were being harassed and murdered, along with outright expulsion from their homes. Oskar's beautiful apartment, appropriated from a Jewish family, overlooked the Planty Park that ringed the picturesque Stary Miasto, or

Old City, of Kraków. This luxurious dwelling also had a view of Wawel Castle, Kraków's most prominent landmark that Hans Frank, the Nazi governor, made his official residence. Oskar lived close to the headquarters of the machinery of terror and occupied a relatively high position in the Nazi hierarchy. This position allowed him to springboard from poverty to wealth, from prison to prominence, and it was all done on the backs of Jews and Poles. Oskar did not come to Poland to help anyone except himself. He thrived in his job as an intelligence officer and used his position to enhance his wealth and prestige. He simply hoped to leave Poland a man of incredible wealth.

Raising Schindler

☐ If you look around at the people who perform the dangerous and difficult jobs in this world—fire fighters, demolition experts, military personnel, machinery operators, roofers, emergency room staff—you will find a much higher percentage of ADHDers and different learners than in the general population.

☐ Children—and adults, for that matter—with a need for risk taking or adventure need to be taught and mentored in unique ways. They need to have their gifts honored and respected, but also require people who can patiently teach them about the importance of consequences and who understand the fact that their brains may make it hard for them to control impulses. So often, children with these gifts are labeled as bad and shunted to the classroom's, and society's, margins. We need to bring them back from the margins so that the world can fully benefit from their incredible aptitudes.

☐ Again, you have to go to school on the brain. The whole ball of wax, gifts and liabilities, comes down to differences in the brain. A child or adult with diabetes is compassionately taught how to eat differently and to learn appropriate monitoring and self-care. People like Oskar Schindler need to be lovingly instructed about their way of being so that they do not feel bad about themselves and so that they understand the unique talents that they bring to life. You must first learn about the ADHD brain, how differences in cerebral structure and functioning lead to problem behaviors, and what you can do to channel your loved one's talents in positive directions.

☐ Mindset is everything. How you think about your ADHD loved one will determine how you respond. When you fill yourself with scientific understanding of ADHD, rather than popular and incorrect notions, you will slowly develop the capacity to respond instead of react. To fully embody this approach, you must make it a daily practice and find people and methods to give yourself plenty of support.

NOTES

1 Oskar came out of prison ready for adventure, and the record indicates he was looking forward to spying once again for the Third Reich. He went right back into action and was quickly transferred to a town on the Polish border, primed to gather intelligence for Hitler's next big move.

2 This is dialogue crafted from the historical record, designed to create a more flowing narrative. Emilie widely discussed the changes that occurred in Oskar during the war.

3 This name is my creation.

4 Schindler, E., 46-47. While Oskar tried to reassure Emilie, she continued to have intense fear about the intense events taking shape around her.

5 Oskar, like his fellow Sudetens, had the unmistakable sense that his ethnic group was treated as second-class citizens. This crafted exchange reflects that reality.

6 The record is clear as to these points. Numerous acquaintances of Oskar's attest to these statements.

7 Heydrich and his cronies in the SS believed they were indeed helping humanity by murdering the Jews. Heydrich's wife was a true-believing Nazi and supported her husband's "work." I depict a conversation between them to offer a stark contrast of conversations between Schindler and Emilie.

8 I took some license to cobble together this section of Heydrich's speech, utilizing these two resources. "Reinhard Heydrich," Holocaust Encyclopedia, United States Holocaust Memorial Museum. Online. Available at http://www.ushmm.org/wlc/en/article.php?ModuleId=10007406; Gerwarth, R. (2011). *Hitler's Hangman: The Life of Heydrich*. Yale University Press: New Haven, CT.

9 This quote is one I have put together from multiple speeches of Himmler. He and his Nazi cronies firmly believed in the superiority of the Aryans, and this belief formed the basis of a twisted and destructive "spirituality." The religiosity of Nazism is one of the least appreciated phenomena of the philosophy. For more on this, see the video series *The Occult History of the Third Reich*, which goes a long way toward elucidating this reality in a thorough as well as entertaining manner.

10 German-speaking people around the whole of Europe received a steady stream of propaganda telling them they were the world's preeminent and superior "race."

11 O'Neil, Pemper, Crowe.

12 For this exchange between Schindler and Scherner, I made use of O'Neil, Pemper, and Crowe.

13 Discussions surrounding the fate of the Jews took place at the highest levels of the Third Reich for years, with many different solutions proposed. At one point the idea was floated that the Jews would be sent to Madagascar, for example. The dialogue in this paragraph is spliced together from various sources containing the actual words of the three Nazis involved.

14 See www.nizkor.org; Gerwarth, R. (2011). *Hitler's Hangman: The Life of Heydrich*. New Haven, CT: Yale University Press; and Nelson, S. (2014). "Heinrich Himmler's Private Letters Published In German Newspaper," NPR.org. Online. Available at http://www.npr.org/sections/thetwo-way/2014/01/26/266698688/heinrich-himmlers-private-letters-published-in-german-newspaper.

15 Gerwarth, R. (2011). *Hitler's Hangman: The Life of Heydrich*. New Haven, CT: Yale University Press.

16 Emilie Schindler wrote about the ongoing and constant revelations that occurred, slowly revealing the truth of the horrors then taking place, amidst rumors of monstrous acts taking place just thirty or so miles from Kraków in Auschwitz.

17 Oskar never got used to the brutality he saw around him. He was intimately acquainted with many of Kraków's Jews and was completely aware of what was hap-

pening to them. He tried to look the other way, largely in the name of good business, but the weight of the horrors eventually overwhelmed him and transformed his life's purpose.

18 The 1930s had not been kind to Oskar. He spent a good deal of that decade unemployed, getting in trouble with the law, and languishing in prison. He was not for the most part in a sufficient mental place to pay attention to world affairs.

19 Again, as the war progressed, Oskar went from skepticism of the Nazis to outright contempt and scorn.

20 Gerwarth.

21 Ibid.

22 Ibid.

23 Oskar held the Nazis in contempt, and expressed this to those closest to him on numerous occasions.

24 In conversations with those around him, Oskar frequently made distinctions of different kinds of Germans.

25 Oskar's visit to the embassy in Turkey is well documented (O'Neil, Crowe).

26 Oskar seems to have taken pride in his ability to outwit the Nazis.

27 Hoza, B., Mrug, S., Peklham, W., Greiner, A., & Gnagy, E. (2003). A friendship intervention for children with Attention Deficit/Hyperactivity Disorder: Preliminary findings. *Journal of Attention Disorders*, Vol. 6, 86-98.

28 Dang, L., Samanez-Larkin, G., Young, J., Cowan, R., Kessler, R., and Zald, D. (2014). Caudate asymmetry is related to attentional impulsivity and an objective measure of ADHD-like attentional problems in healthy adults. *Brain Structure and Function*. Jan;221(1):277-86

29 Hitler and Canaris did share an antipathy and mistrust for the Soviet Union, a fact that initially created a bond of trust. Canaris, however, came to see Hitler as a threat to Germany, a man likely to lead the nation to ruin.

30 This conversation between Hitler and Canaris is spliced together from things both men said. I relied heavily for this dialogue on Bassett, R. (2005). *Hitler's Spy Chief*. London: Orion House; and Shirer, W. (1960). *The Rise and Fall of the Third Reich*. New York: Simon and Shuster.

31 Ibid.

32 Bassett, R. (2005). *Hitler's Spy Chief*. London: Orion House.

33 Ibid.

34 Bassett, 178.

35 Bassett, Shirer.

36 Bassett and Shirer. This excerpt is an amalgam of a few separate exchanges.

37 The BBC interviewed Karl Wolff for its series, *The World at War*. This is my source for this information.

38 Bassett, 221.

39 Bassett.

40 Bassett.

41 Ibid.

42 Crowe, D. (2004). *Oskar Schindler: The Untold Account of His Life, Wartime Activities, and the True Story Behind the List*. New York: Basic Books, 173.

43 Strzelecki, A. (1998). "The plunder of the victim and their corpses," in *Anatomy of the Auschwitz Death Camp* (Edited by Gutman, Y., and Berenbaum, M.). Bloomington: Indiana University Press.

44 Strzelecki.

45 Ibid.

46 This point was highlighted over and over again by my guide during my first tour of Auschwitz.

47 Ibid.

48 This section relied on Crowe, O'Neil, and Bassett. I used these sources to craft the words.

49 Gerwarth.

50 Strzelecki.

Chapter 4 Falling into Insanity

In individuals, insanity is rare;
but in groups, parties, nations and epochs, it is the rule.

—Friedrich Nietzsche

Corruption was King

"THIS IS A WORLD OF OPPOSITES,"[1] Oskar wrote to Emilie from Kraków in early 1940. "Everything is contrary to human reason and common sense. The most hard-working people are thrown into the street, their businesses and homes stolen out from under them. Good people are branded as evil, and evil people think themselves virtuous. Every single day I see something that shocks me." The hard-to-believe fact is that Oskar continued to be shocked throughout the war as Nazi atrocities seemed to know no bounds. The upside-down world of the General Government in Poland nevertheless provided him with unexpected opportunities. He told Emilie, "Some have called me Schindler the Swindler. Maybe they were right, and maybe that's why I know how to get along with these Nazis. What's going on in Poland right now is way beyond swindling. It is as if the demons of hell have been let loose on Earth."[2]

Hitler and his governor in Poland, Hans Frank,[3] made it government policy to unleash Nazi wrath. "Our goal in the General Government is to purify this land of Poles and Jews and make it fit for German settlement,"[4] Frank said in a speech to his Nazi underlings in 1940 in the courtyard of Wawel Castle. "The area of the General Government must become a pure German colonized land. Gentlemen, I must ask you to rid yourselves of all feelings of pity. We must annihilate the Jews, and enslave the Poles. The Reich must expand." As part of Frank's vision, millions of Jews, and certainly millions more non-Jewish occupied people, had their homes, businesses, possessions, and money confiscated. Once in control of Poland, Frank and his fellow Nazi collaborators created a world of insane chaos in which they upended every rule, procedure, tradition, law, and practice of the local population and abandoned human decency.

As with almost every crime the Nazis perpetrated, they did not proceed in a haphazard fashion. They systematized crime; an entire bureaucracy grew up around stealing from conquered peoples, especially the Jews. This was started right in Germany before the war even began. The Finanzamt (Tax Office) of the German government shared tax records that the Gestapo used to seize the assets of German Jews, starting with those who had emigrated. In 1937, Schindler's nemesis, Heydrich,[5] became intimately involved with this process. Wealthier German Jews, under Heydrich's leadership, were actually encouraged to leave Germany so that their property could be easily confiscated; those who left Germany saved their own lives but were forced to surrender almost all of their property and pay enormous fees to the German government for the privilege of leaving. Sadly, since many of these folks fled to countries that Germany eventually conquered, the Nazis ended up murdering a high percentage of them anyway.

Jews march with bundles of belongings out of the Kraków ghetto in 1943.
United States Holocaust Memorial Museum, courtesy of Instytut Pamieci Narodowej

"We're in at the ground floor," Oskar wrote to Emilie. "For the first time in my life, I am at the top of the heap looking down. I can see exactly what needs to happen and I intend to make us very rich indeed."[6] Oskar had instant access to the vast wheels of a Nazi bureaucracy that was hungry for the money it could make by confiscating and then selling stolen property. On October 19, 1939, Hermann Göring, Hitler's second in command, set up the Main Trusteeship Office for the East, which oversaw the structured theft. "We must work hard to ensure that this mass transfer of property proceeds in an organized fashion,"[7] Göring said. "For the good of the Reich, we will systematize the forfeiture of Polish and Jewish property and arrange for the efficient sale and redistribution of that property to Germans, with the proceeds of course going back to the government in Berlin." Oskar was one of those Germans who managed to score stolen property under Göring's system, but even with his get-rich-at-any-cost mindset, Oskar had misgivings. "Some of the people here are like vultures,"[8] Oskar wrote Emilie in December 1939, "hovering, primed to pick the carcass clean. Some days I do feel a bit guilty, but I did not create this situation and I am not going to squander this once-in-a-lifetime opportunity."

While he went forward with his plans to enrich himself, Oskar's humanity remained intact. He not only helped Jews very early on in the war, but the Poles as well. "The Poles also suffer enormously under the Nazis," he told Emilie. "They not only desecrate synagogues and Hebrew books of prayer, but they are also looting Polish public buildings. They deface or knock down Polish schools, monuments, museums, and government buildings." Among conquered peoples, the Poles occupied an unenviable position because the Nazis considered them particularly inferior and their lands as a suitable place for Germans to settle. Hoping to colonize Polish territory, the Nazis aimed to destroy the structures of Polish government and culture, as well as the Polish intelligentsia, such as politicians, clergy, teachers, and university professors. They sent many Polish professors, who were viewed as potential resistance leaders, straight away to concentration camps. They quickly went about the process of enslaving the Poles, sending millions of them into Germany to labor on farms and in factories. Ironically, enslavement of the Poles would ultimately help save the Schindler Jews. As Poles were forced to work in Germany, armaments production in Poland suffered a manpower shortage, opening a gap that some Jewish workers were able to fill, if only temporarily.

From the very beginning of his plan to take over Poland, Hitler envisioned mass murder and theft. In a speech to his generals a week before he invaded Poland, he made his mind-set painstakingly clear:

> Our strength consists in our speed and in our bru-tality. Genghis Khan led millions of women and children to slaughter—with premeditation and a happy heart. History sees in him solely the founder of a state. It's a matter of indifference to me what a weak western European civilization will say about me. I have issued the command—and I'll have any-body who utters but one word of criticism executed by a firing squad—that our war aim does not consist in reaching certain lines, but in the physical destruc-tion of the enemy. Accordingly, I have placed my death-head formation in readiness—for the pres-ent only in the East—with orders to them to send to death mercilessly and without compassion, men, women, and children of Polish origin and language. Only thus shall we gain the living space which we need.[9]

While Poles and Jews had six years of terror awaiting them, Schindler and other war profiteers began to amass un-told wealth.

With a Little Help from his Friends

"If I cannot succeed in Kraków," Oskar wrote to Emilie in 1939, "I will never succeed."[10] Bargain-basement prices for business-es along with a cheap and abundant supply of labor awaited Oskar in Kraków. He stalked the Trusteeship Office in the city, combing through records to find a business for himself and his agents. Oskar first set up one of his Abwehr subordinate agents, Joseph Aue, in a formerly Jewish-owned business.[11,12] Oskar introduced him to acquaintances in the office, and these highly placed individuals shepherded Aue through the process. Aue took over a Jewish import/export business, the chief accountant of which was Yitzhak Stern, a man who would play a significant role in helping save the Schindler Jews.[13] Stern impressed Aue, who eventually introduced him to Schindler; Oskar was also immediately impressed by this quietly strong man and inclined to follow his recommendations. "You must," Stern advised, "stay informed on Nazi policies because they can change on a daily basis. And do not become a trustee of any Jewish business; you must become the owner, otherwise you will be much more beholden to the German government. I do not imagine, Mr. Schindler, that you are a man who wants the government telling him what to do."[14] Stern seemed to immediately grasp Oskar's character and disposition. In spite of the fact that Jews had to be wary of any contact with Germans, Stern quickly warmed to Schindler. Convinced of the wisdom of Stern's words at that early meeting, Oskar displayed a rare spate of patience as he poured through documents to find just the right company.

Through a friend, Major von Kohrab of the Abwehr, Oskar met a Jewish businessman, Abraham Bankier, the Jewish former owner of a company called Rekord, which produced enamelware.[15] After extensively consulting with Stern and Bankier, Oskar purchased this company and changed its name to Deutsche Emailenwaren Fabrik (DEF), sometimes simply referred to as Emalia. While the factory was transferred to Oskar in early 1940, he did not become the full owner until the fall of 1941. His initial workforce at the factory was made up exclusively of Poles until mid-1941, when Schindler hired his first Jewish workers.

While Jews provided Oskar with an almost free source of labor, he was also the beneficiary of free, highly skilled business consultants. Oskar found something in these Jewish businessmen that he had never quite experienced: total support. Before becoming a spy for the Abwehr, Schindler had had no

Entrance to Emalia facility, 1943 or 1944. *United States Holocaust Memorial Museum, courtesy of Leopold Page Photographic Collection*

career path and held and lost a ceaseless stream of jobs. His business ventures had all failed miserably. Yet he used his influence among the Nazis to land a good-sized manufacturing operation. He possessed no experience or training in this area and, like almost all ADHDers I know, lacked the organization, follow through, and planning needed to run such a complex enterprise. However, he still managed to make some great business decisions, the most notable of which was hiring Abraham Bankier. "Bankier is a business guru,"[16] Oskar frequently told friends. "Yes, he understands manufacturing, marketing, and sales, but more importantly, he knows the black market, where 80 percent of what we make actually gets sold." The black market occupies a place of the highest importance in the Schindler saga because the war created scarcity for certain products, like chocolate, cigarettes, liquor, and other luxury items. Bankier's success at procuring such items provided Oskar's operation with a "certain panache."[17] Schindler obtained these goods and then showered them on his Nazi contacts. Schindler was the spring of luxury and even many die-hard Nazi zealots did not want to see that source dry up. "If they kept me in jail," Schindler told Bankier, "they would go without German cigarettes and chocolate. Their hedonism is my get-out-of-jail-free card."[18]

The factory was in many respects merely a cover, although an absolutely essential one to deflect attention on their black market activities. Bankier and Schindler excelled at making their operation look legitimate. Perhaps one of the factors that helped Schindler stay focused was that his business was not really legitimate. That would have been no fun for Oskar. He liked breaking the rules, and Bankier provided him with a plausible façade. "Schindler and Bankier were an unlikely pair running an unlikely operation," a close friend of Oskar's, Janka Olszewska,[19] said. "They made their very illegitimate operation look legitimate, which was quite a feat indeed, given what was going on in Poland at that time. Without both of them, the operation would have failed."[20] In Spielberg's movie, Bankier only receives one mention. In the scene where the Jews are lining up to try to get a work permit card, the Blauschein, Yitzhak Stern hands the Nazi clerk a list of people who were to work at Schindler's factory. He tells the clerk that these are "signed by Mr. Bankier and myself."[21] Most probably for cinematic reasons, director Steven Spielberg chose to let the character Yitzhak Stern be a composite character of Abraham Bankier, Mieczylaw Pemper, and the real Yitzhak Stern. All three men played crucial roles in the Schindler saga; without all of them, Schindler's operation would not have prospered and he would never been able to endure to the end of the war with his Jewish workforce intact. Again, Oskar had highly competent, round-the-clock support, something he did not enjoy before the war, or after.

"Stern urged me to buy the factory, instead of just becoming a German trustee,"[22] Oskar told a reporter after the war. "If I had not followed this advice, I never would have owned a factory that I could then have moved along with my Jewish workers. They would have been murdered along with the other six million." Oskar continued, "Stern counseled me to buy the Rekord Company and approved of my connection with Abraham Bankier. Bankier, in turn, ran the business with an incredibly high level of efficiency and effectiveness, and was also a master of buying and selling on the black market. I could leave for weeks at a time, and Bankier would keep things humming along beautifully."[23] Toward the end of 1941, Oskar's prowess on the black market caught up to him. He was actually arrested by the Gestapo for his black market activities, but in a pattern that was to be oft repeated, his secretary made a few phone calls to his powerful friends, which quickly led to his release.

After Oskar spent a few days in the Gestapo prison, he and Bankier went right back to making large amounts of money. Schindler did not have much to do with Stern after their initial dealings in 1939, but when the Płaszów slave labor camp was opened in 1943, Stern worked closely with the camp administration. His contacts inside the camp greatly complemented Schindler's efforts to save his Jewish workers, and he also introduced Oskar to Jewish relief agencies. Mieczylaw (Mietek) Pemper also worked in the camp administration and was essentially the personal assistant to camp commandant, Amon Göth. Pemper occupies an equally important position to that of Bankier and Stern. Pemper had access inside the camp to classified German documents, and he possessed a photographic memory. He provided Schindler with crucial details, including the timing of important events, that helped

ADHD: Impaired Learning

When we find something rewarding and pleasurable, we seek to repeat it, and discomfort generally motivates us to stop an experience and avoid it in the future. One facet of ADHD is that the condition represents impairment in this reward-learning loop. Experiencing a negative consequence from a behavior does not always lead, in an ADHD individual, to the ability to prevent that behavior in the future. Likewise, positive reinforcement also functions atypically in ADHD people. While the brain is a very complex organ that we still struggle to comprehend, science makes a good case that anomalies in the functioning of certain neurotransmitters, like dopamine, play a significant role in this impaired reward mechanism in ADHD. Many of the drugs that work well in ADHD people have an impact on dopamine and norepinephrine pathways in the brain. Dopamine is a neurotransmitter that is particularly involved in the reward circuitry of the brain, but more specifically, this neurochemical is about survival, doing something because it feels crucial to our continued existence. Dopamine also plays a key role in moti-

Oskar continued to thrive in business and ultimately save his employees. Oskar, an ADHD genius, could not have done what he did without these three men whom I refer to as his ADHD coaches. Oskar Schindler possessed a genius that required external catalysts to properly function. With the right support, so many ADHD failures could easily be turned into success. The trouble with many of us with ADHD is that we usually have an overwhelming impulse to go it alone, something I still struggle with.

vation, which is often impaired in ADHDers. A variant of the dopamine receptor gene, DRD4, found in 29 percent of ADHDers,
has been associated with greater impulsivity and hyperactivity.
The way that the dopamine system works in ADHDers means
that we have an atypical way of motivating ourselves, often
needing much more intensity than the average person to allow us to function "normally." We have different configurations
of neurotransmitter receptors and transporters than non-ADHD
people. It is important to keep in mind that ADHD is a condition governed by the neurobiological environment of the brain.
Clearly, Oskar Schindler battled a lack of motivation. The potential for future reward was generally not enough for him to mud-
dle through details and stay engaged. He grew bored of some
business ventures after only a few weeks. He was not a bad person, nor was he innately lazy. He had a brain that made some aspects of life extraordinarily challenging. Please understand that
these remarks merely scratch the surface of understanding the
ADHD brain.

Oskar blossomed with proper support and floundered
for the rest of his life without it. As previously stated, one line
from the movie, "not the work, not the work ... the presentation," gets to the heart of Oskar Schindler. He had no patience
for detail, and no patience, period.[24] The inability to delay reward defines ADHD to a large extent. Children with ADHD
will almost always choose a small, short-term reward over a
significantly larger long-term reward, and this trait often fol-
lows individuals, like Oskar and the author of this book, into

adulthood. Doing well in school and in most jobs requires the delay of reward. An individual has to have a brain that can singularly concentrate on the topic at hand and continue to focus over long periods of time, even though the reward may not come for three or four months, in the case of school, and perhaps three to four years in the case of a job, or with someone attending college or graduate school. That individual must also be adept at filtering out extraneous information and stimuli, so that he or she does not get distracted and absorbed in other activities that do not help achieve a goal, whether it is school-related or simply a household chore. World War II treated Oskar to an environment in which he could do the things he excelled at while others handled the details and advised him on the right courses of action. Without the war, Stern, Pemper, and Bankier probably would not have given Oskar the time of day. But during that time of tribulation, he was an imperfect angel who had exactly the skills they needed to keep themselves and twelve hundred others alive.

Outwitting Evil.

Undoubtedly, Oskar came to Kraków a greedy opportunist, willing to employ any advantage to help himself to the plunder the Nazis had amassed from pillaging Jewish and Polish property. The unbridled brutality of the Nazis progressively weighed on him, though even early on he showed no appetite for cruelty. In fact, from his first days in Poland, evidence exists that he worked against the policies of the Third Reich. On December 3, 1939, Schindler visited Stern with the expressed intention of warning him about coming danger.[25] Oskar had learned that the Nazis were going to surround the neighborhood of Kazimierz, the Jewish Quarter, and arrest and perhaps murder Jews, in addition to stealing their property.[26] "Get yourself and your family out of Kazimierz on that day, or you may go missing,"[27] he told Stern. Warning Jews about impending actions could certainly have landed Oskar in jail, or even a concentration camp. Later that same month, Schindler saved a Jewish man, Leon Bosak, from arrest by the Gestapo by enlisting the help of a friend in the SS.[28] For the first year or so of his factory's operation, Schindler also saved dozens of Poles from being forcibly shipped to Germany by employing more of them than he actually needed to run his factory.[29] These facts show that Schindler exhibited a humanitarian impulse from the early days of his time in Kraków; he helped Jews and Poles alike. From the moment of his arrival in Kraków, he showed a willingness to risk his own well-being to help others. But to continue doing this, he had to play a double game, walking a tight rope between caring for the Jewish people and acting like a good old Nazi.

Survival of the Jews lay between the ebb and flow of two parallel currents, one bent on the total destruction of the Jews, and the other mindful of the need to use them to relieve the labor shortage in Germany's armaments industries. Himmler, Heydrich, and Hitler considered it sacrilegious to think that Jews could play a vital role in Germany's wartime economy. Governor Hans Frank, following Hitler's directives, told his subordinates in Poland that "the Jews were to be removed from all trades, especially from trade with agricultural products and other foodstuffs. Their rations will be kept at starvation levels. The Jew has no place in the Reich economy."[30] Early in the war, with one nation after another quickly falling to the German Blitzkrieg, or "lightning war," this view won out. As the German armies sped through the Soviet Union in the summer of 1941, the Einsaztgruppen, extermination squads, followed behind, organizing mass shootings of the Jews in those areas. The Nazis at this time were only interested in killing the Jews, and saw no use for them as laborers. German officer Otto Ohlendorf ran one of these murder brigades, Einsatzgruppe

D. Questioned at his war crimes trial, he gave a description of how this type of action took place:

> The Einsatz unit would enter a village or town and order the prominent Jewish citizens to call together all the Jews for the purpose of "resettlement." They were instructed to hand over their valuables and shortly before execution to surrender their outer clothing. They were transported to the place of execution, usually an anti-tank ditch, in trucks—always only as many as could be executed immediately. In this way it was attempted to keep the span of time from the moment in which the victims knew what was about to happen to them until the time of their actual execution as short as possible. Then they were shot, kneeling or standing, by firing squads in a military manner and the corpses thrown into the ditch.[31]

The Nazis killed over a million Jews using this method. This murderous spree gives an idea of the type of psychotic zeal Oskar Schindler was up against. As the German armies rolled on to what they assumed would be ultimate victory, the speed and scope of killing Jews quickened its pace.

In early 1942, Heydrich convened a meeting at Wannsee, an upscale suburb of Berlin, to come up with what was being termed the Final Solution. By this point, Heydrich and the upper echelon of the Nazis agreed that term meant extermination. Heydrich began the meeting by stating that "approximately eleven million Jews will be involved in the final solution of the European Jewish question."[32] He impressed his guests by facilely citing the numbers of Jews known to be living in each country, and even including specific breakdowns of various regions. This information had been provided to him in a brief that had been prepared by Lt. Colonel Adolf Eichmann, another of the Holocaust's great villains, one who prided himself on being thorough and efficient. The Nazis went about this murderous process in an extraordinarily methodical manner. The murdering of Europe's Jews after that meeting took on its well-known industrial character; the Nazis essentially designed—for the first time in human history—factories of death that were supplied with murder victims by the vast German rail network.

Out of this meeting, now known as the Wannsee Conference, an ominously innovative plan of action was initiated. Called Aktion Reinhard, this new and supremely destructive phase of the Nazi campaign of extermination centered around three death camps: Treblinka, Sobibór, and Belżec, all located in Poland with easy access to rail lines. In less than two years, this operation murdered over two million Jews, Gypsies, Poles, and Soviet prisoners of war. Unlike their more infamous cousin, Auschwitz-Birkenau, these three killing centers did not have huge labor camps attached to them. Everyone, save a precious few who worked in the camps or escaped, died within hours of arrival.

Kraków did not escape Aktion Reinhard. First of all, on March 3, 1941, the Germans had established the Kraków ghetto, a walled section of the city where fifteen thousand Jews were crammed into an area that had previously housed three thousand people. The Germans constructed the walls to look like Jewish tombstones, a move that foreshadowed the coming horror. Concentrating the Jews in this way made rounding them up for transport/deportation quite easy.

On May 28, 1942, the ghetto was completely sealed off. Jews deemed fit for work received a stamp on their identity card. Those without a stamp, or who had perhaps left their identity card at home, were at risk of being selected for the transport. Schindler tried to keep as many of his workers as possible in the factory, hoping to save them from the Nazi ter-

People near a section of the Kraków ghetto wall, which was built to resemble tombstones, 1941. *United States Holocaust Memorial Museum, courtesy of David Werdiger*

ror that had begun. German soldiers roamed the streets, demanding to see identity cards, and even Jewish ghetto police participated in perpetrating this horror. They corralled those unfortunate enough to have been caught in the central square of the ghetto. Random shootings and ravenous theft of Jewish valuables accompanied this event. On June 1, 1942, the first transport left Kraków in route to Belżec, a death camp that used diesel engines to pump carbon monoxide into the gas chambers. On June 3, fourteen of Schindler's workers were rounded up and forced onto the next transport. This group included Abraham Bankier, the plant manager. Schindler boldly intervened and obtained release for all fourteen. Pulling Jews off of death camp-bound trains just did not happen in the Third Reich. Schindler had to muster every ounce of charisma from his being, bribe zealous Nazi clerks, and threaten reprisals from his high-placed friends. His success in saving Jews who had already been slated for death, who were already loaded on cattle cars, shows the power, audacity, and genius—if not recklessness—of Oskar Schindler. While successful, such steps on Schindler's part progressively brought a higher level of SS and Gestapo scrutiny.

On June 4, 1942, the SS deported seven thousand more of Kraków Jews, people who thought they were being "resettled in the east." A dentist from Kraków, Dr. Bachner, found himself on a subsequent transport to this death camp, and managed to escape Belżec's gas chamber by slipping away and standing in a latrine pit in the camp for three days.[33] He made his way back to Kraków and alerted people to what was going on. Schindler eventually heard Dr. Bachner's story and attempted to see for himself, driving several times to the outskirts of the town of Belżec—which was several hours away—but he was unable to penetrate the cordon of security.[34] "I tried to get close," he told Emilie, "but this backwater town and the area around it were swimming with SS. I couldn't get anywhere near the camp. They're doing something in there that they want to hide from the world. I can tell you this: There is no resettlement going on. Those people are going into that camp and never coming out."[35] This incident goes further to demonstrate Oskar's courage; anyone found even close to the camp would have been shot unless that individual possessed security clearance from someone like Heydrich, Himmler, or Odilo Globocnik, head of Aktion Reinhard.[36] Schindler flirted with disaster to try to find out exactly what was happening to the Jews. Once again, he cheated death, returning to Kraków that summer with an ever-deepening commitment to work against the Nazis. Incidentally, another factory of death, Chełmno, was located north of Kraków. This site used the notorious gassing vans as the instrument of murder. A clerk from that town's council, Stanisław Kaszyński, was arrested by the SS after he tried to get the word out about what the Nazis were doing at Chełmno.[37] They summarily executed him along with his wife a few days later.[38] Oskar narrowly avoided the Kaszyński's fate on numerous occasions.

"Work Was Synonymous with Survival" —Mietek Pemper

As the killing of innocent people increased, Germany's success on the battlefield started to slow. With more Germans needed in the military, the nation experienced a huge scarcity of workers. At first, they tried to solve this problem by importing foreign workers. By the early fall of 1944, over seven-and-a-half million civilian foreigners had been rounded up in their home countries, shoved into boxcars, and shipped to Germany.[39] They were not only forced to work, but also "degraded, beaten, and starved, and often left to die for lack of food, clothing and shelter."[40] The Germans often tore families apart, sending mothers, fathers and children to different parts of Germany to work. Hitler had no moral qualms about these violations, viewing the Slavs as subhuman:

> As for the ridiculous hundred million Slavs, we will mold the best of them to the shape that suits us, and we will isolate the rest of them in their own pigsties; and anyone who talks about cherishing the local inhabitant and civilizing him, goes straight to a concentration camp.[41]

Millions of these unfortunate Slavic slaves shipped to the Reich were from Poland, leaving a consequent labor short-fall in their homeland. Luckily for Schindler—and his Jewish workers—this situation afforded an opening.

Discussions at the highest levels of the Nazi hierarchy frequently centered on the role of Jewish slave laborers in the economy. Purists in the SS, along with Hitler himself, thought it blasphemy to assert that Jewish people played any economic role in the Third Reich. "Our work has been to eliminate the Jew from the Reich economy,"[42] Heydrich told a group of sub-ordinate officers. "If we make a place for Jewish labor in our endeavors, the work we have already done is for naught." Jews had been toiling in the many Nazi work camps, but the death rate remained intentionally high. In some camps, the average inmate lived only a few weeks or months. This death-through-hard-work approach began to become inconvenient as the war wore on. By the end of 1942, Himmler started to send out di-rectives that the death rate in forced-labor camps needed to be significantly reduced, reflecting the German military loss-es against the Soviets that accompanied the grave shortage in able-bodied workers. Still, the Nazis were determined to de-stroy European Jewry, but decided to allow some Jews to live a little longer so that they could serve the German war machine.

Only Jews deemed essential to the war effort received a temporary reprieve from extermination. In December 1942, the Kraków ghetto reflected this disturbing reality: the ghetto was split into two, with one side for essential workers and the other for those who could not work. The reasons for this sep-aration became clear in March 1943, when the SS liquidated the ghetto. Schindler and his Jewish partners tirelessly worked to ensure that his operation met German requirements so that at least his workers would not be the ones rounded up and "resettled," a euphemism that Oskar absolutely understood to mean murder. Factories not considered crucial to the war ef-

fort would be shut down, and Jewish workers in those factories would be sent straight away to Bełżec and later Auschwitz.
Schindler and his inner circle had to constantly reinvent the
operation to avoid being shut down by the Nazis.

Master Manipulator.

Many of Oskar's critics after the war decided to shed light on
his numerous high-ranking Nazi contacts. These folks pointed
out that Oskar paid regular and frequent social visits to many
individuals who were later convicted of war crimes. Multiple
high-ranking members of the SS actually considered Oskar a
friend, these critics pointed out. Yad Vashem, the Israeli organization that gives awards to the "righteous" who assisted the
victims of the Holocaust, received numerous letters asserting
Schindler's guilt by association. Responding to his detractors,
Oskar used his characteristic sarcastic wit: "At that stage in history, it was rather difficult to discuss the fate of Jews with the
chief rabbi of Jerusalem."[43] The irony of the massive criticism
leveled at Schindler is that without his Nazi contacts, and his
ability to move in the highest Nazi circles, he could not have
saved a single Jewish worker, let alone helped Polish people.

His Nazi contacts alerted him, for example, to anti-Jewish
actions of the SS. Time and again, Schindler warned Jewish
inhabitants of Kraków about the actions, and on numerous occasions, he kept his workers in the factory overnight to allow
them to avoid the roundups and indiscriminate killings in the
ghetto.[44] Workers at Emalia lived in the ghetto and were escorted to and from the factory by brutal guards. By early 1943,
Schindler grasped that the Jews were destined for disaster. "If I
build my own camp around the factory,"[45] he told Emilie, "I can
safeguard my workers from daily torment by SS and Ukrainian
guards, prevent summary executions, and actually maintain a
higher level of productivity."[46] Convincing the multiple layers
of Nazi bureaucracy to let him do that invariably required a

Göth with his rifle on the balcony of his villa at the Plaszow concentration camp, 1943. *United States Holocaust Memorial Museum, courtesy of Leopold Page Photographic Collection*

massive outflow of bribes, starting with the commandant of the labor camp, Amon Göth. "Whenever I show up at Göth's office," Oskar said, "I must at the very least have a bottle of cognac, and the commandant has very expensive taste. That's why I do try to visit the camp when I know Göth is away. That makes my visit infinitely less costly."[47] In addition to paying off Göth, Schindler had to bribe his way through numerous and often redundant layers of Nazi bureaucracy and then convince officials at the Armaments Inspectorate, the board that oversaw all wartime production.

Oskar did not have to go too far, however, to convince his friends in the Armaments Inspectorate that a sub-camp at his factory made logical sense. It didn't hurt that Maximillian

Schindler, a high-ranking general in the Armaments Inspectorate, was presumed by many to be a relative of Oskar's. While this was not the case, Oskar, ever the gifted deceiver, carefully let people think it was true.[48] General Schindler was a top player in Oskar's scheme. The Armaments Inspectorate oversaw everything related to weapons production. General Schindler was one of the good guys without whose support Oskar's whole operation would have crumbled. Oskar's contacts with Admiral Canaris and the Abwehr certainly helped him in forging a relationship with the general, but the two men seem also to have been friends by the end of the war. "Having a lieutenant-general presumed to be one's relative,"[49] Oskar told Stern, "helps significantly to smooth negotiations."

Oskar had to bribe and schmooze armament officials in Berlin as well as in Poland, police officials in Kraków, the SS, the concentration camp administration, and of course, Amon Göth, the Nazi beast who ran the Płaszów work camp that housed Oskar's Jewish workers. Göth had at first strongly opposed Oskar getting his own satellite camp, but Oskar won him over to such an extent that Göth eventually went personally to Julian Scherner, a member of the SS and police chief of Kraków, and persuaded him to move forward with Schindler's plan.

Oskar had done such an outstanding job outsmarting the commandant of Płaszów that even after the war was over, Göth considered Schindler his friend and asked him to testify as a character witness at his war crimes trial.[50] Oskar declined, much to Göth's utter shock and dismay.[51] Göth stands as one of the most barbaric and bestial of all the Holocaust's villains. While most labor and death camp commandants did not directly participate in murdering their Jewish victims, Göth killed at least eight thousand people with his own hand or under his direct, explicit orders.[52] Göth regularly shot inmates of the work camp from the comfort of his own bedroom, claiming to pick off those who appeared to be working too slowly. Upon spotting him at his window with his high-powered rifle, inmates would scurry in panic out of his field of view. Unfortunately, they could not escape his large dogs, Ralf and Rolf, who Göth had trained to tear inmates apart, an act which became a regular feature at the camp.

Göth came to Kraków after having been a chief assistant to Odilo Globocnik, the head of Aktion Reinhard. In this position, he made regular visits to Treblinka, Sobibór, and Belżec, in addition to participating in numerous murderous rampages in Jewish ghettoes across Poland. In the Tarnów ghetto, he shot a six-year-old boy, who came out from his hiding place on Göth's assurance and calls that nothing would happen to him.[53] He helped supervise the killing of thousands when the Kraków ghetto was liquidated on March 13, 1943, murdering those unfit or unable to work and carting off the rest of them, between eight thousand and ten thousand people, to be worked to death at Płaszów. Even Oskar's workers were forced into Płaszów, but after just seven weeks, work was finished on the sub-camp around the Schindler factory, and Oskar's whole workforce moved in. Those lucky enough to work for Oskar Schindler now enjoyed a relatively secure existence, absent most of the brutality and deprivation experienced by those under Göth's direct control. Richard Rechen, a Jewish man who worked for Schindler, put it this way:

> It was like falling onto another planet. Director Schindler came into the garage where I was working. He greets me and gives me his hand. He told me not to be afraid. He said he had heard that I was a good mechanic and invited me to come to the Emalia factory where I would never be hungry.[54]

By contrast, those under Göth's daily regimen of cruelty lived each moment not knowing if it would be their last.

Starvation killed many inmates there. The rations in all German camps were incredibly meager, but inmates in Płaszów had less to eat because Göth took food destined for prisoners and sold it on the black market, pocketing the money. Those who knew him well talked about the enjoyment he achieved from making others suffer. Josef Bau, who was eventually saved by Schindler, endured and observed the depths of Göth's inhumanity:

> At one morning parade, in the presence of all the prisoners, Göth shot a Jew because, as he complained, the man was too tall. Then, as the man lay dying, he urinated on him. Once he caught a boy who was sick from diarrhea and was unable to restrain himself. Göth forced him to eat all the excrement and then shot him.[55]

The trouble with describing Göth is that the anecdotes of those who experienced and witnessed his cruelty could fill volumes. The important point for this work is that he was a man of enormous evil whom Schindler duped into supporting his efforts to save his workers. Without winning over Göth, none of Oskar's efforts would have come to fruition. The successful deception of Göth was the fulcrum of Oskar's ultimate triumph. Yes, Schindler eventually bribed and outwitted scores of Nazi officials. Göth, however, exercised immediate control over Oskar's operation and had the position and standing to convince his superiors of the value of Schindler's endeavors.

Shrewd in deception, Oskar maintained the ruse that he liked Göth until the war was over, even after Göth was arrested and detained by the SS for theft and corruption in the fall of 1944. Oskar went so far as to arrange for the transport of all Göth's booty, the huge treasure trove of stolen Jewish wealth he had amassed. Oskar had these items shipped to his new factory in Czechoslovakia and kept them for Göth until the end of the war. Several witnesses have testified that Schindler feared that

Göth could have easily shut down the whole operation. His cooperation and good will, Oskar reasoned, were crucial. Mietek Pemper said that from at least March 1943, Schindler took every conceivable step to convince Göth that he was his loyal friend and fellow Nazi. Oskar exploited his contacts with Göth and other high-level Nazis to protect his Jewish workers.[56]

Essential to the War

Among the many examples of masterful manipulation stands Oskar's massive efforts to make certain that his factory continued its designation as essential to the war effort, or *siegentscheidend*, which means "crucial for victory" in German.[57] As German troops progressively recoiled around Stalingrad in the Soviet Union in late 1942 and early 1943, starving and dying along the way, factories in Poland that produced military items could conceivably maintain their operations and thus their Jewish workforce. Crucial items were in short supply, as was the labor to produce those items. The Armaments Inspectorate enforced strict guidelines, however, and regularly visited manufacturing facilities as well as forced-labor camps.

In the fall of 1943, high-level talks in the Armaments Inspectorate and the Economic Office led to many smaller camps being closed. Schindler would have been ignorant of these developments had he not been introduced, through Stern, to Pemper, another man with quiet courage and a photographic memory. He slipped under the Nazi radar and was one of Göth's most trusted assistants. He regularly read the top-secret dispatches and communiques that came through Göth's office and passed on crucial information to Schindler. Having essentially memorized dozens of highly sensitive and classified documents, Pemper was an incredible witness in several war crimes trials, including that of Amon Göth.[58] His access to the inner workings of the Nazi Concentration Camp

Administration supplied Oskar with information without which his operation would certainly have been shut down.[59]

As of June 1943, two million of the Jews living in the General Government of Poland had been murdered, leaving roughly one hundred twenty thousand working in fifty or so labor camps, including Płaszów.[60] Schindler's Jewish workers, along with those in Płaszów, clung to life by a thread. In the early fall of 1943, Pemper and Stern became aware of the danger that Płaszów could close down. They, in concert with Oskar, took initiative to put together production tables that highlighted the potential for the factories of the camp to produce military items, deceptively giving the impression that the items were already in production. Göth, also wanting to preserve the camp and his life of luxury and control, took these meticulously prepared documents to a meeting at which the fate of the labor camps around Poland was discussed. Pemper and Stern produced a report of such incredible detail that it did the trick of convincing the higher-ups that Płaszów could make significant contributions to the war. Officials from the Armaments Inspectorate then made a visit to Schindler's operations.

Schindler was the guide of their factory tour, with Stern accompanying them. "Stern had such a serious and almost scholarly presence,"[61] Schindler said, "that the Armaments Inspectors paid close attention to whatever he said. He provided such a maddeningly long list of production details that I believe he significantly bolstered the case for Płaszów remaining open when the inspectors came to tour the camp and repeatedly interrogated him." Schindler complemented Stern and Pemper's efforts by arranging for the electricity to go out as the inspectors toured his factory. Schindler was convinced that the relative darkness inside the plant made his machinery and operation seem much more impressive. Also, instead of

Hooked on the Negative[65]

Parents of young people with ADHD often report that their children spend more time and energy making up and maintaining lies than it would take to simply complete their homework. Frustrated, these parents do not understand that deception activates our brains in a way that homework does not. We do it because it turns on our brains, and yes, we seriously hate most of the boring, repetitive, and inane homework assignments as well. We develop an almost instinctual urge to avoid those sorts of tasks. Doing them becomes hateful. The ADHD brain functions poorly during the performance of low-intensity activities. Brain scans conclusively show that when an ADHD individual attempts to concentrate on a boring, low-intensity task, activity in the frontal regions of the brain actually decreases. Negative and high-intensity stimuli, however, cause the ADHD brain to turn on, to function more optimally. For this reason, many ADHDers are unconsciously drawn to negativity because it helps their brains. This can have a destructive impact on relationships, family, and career, but as Oskar Schindler shows, it can have powerfully beneficial "side effects" as well. Some of the most innovative as well as destructive things in this world happen after an ADHD person tells him or herself, "I'm bored." Oskar was never bored during the war, allowing his brain to function optimally so that he could continually find solutions to problems of life and death.

viewing the operation firsthand, the inspectors were forced to rely on silver-tongued Schindler's narration.[62]

By this time, Schindler had already begun to produce grenade parts, allowing his manufacturing operation to receive the designation of essential for victory. Without Stern and Pemper supplying him with inside information, Oskar would have remained unaware of changes in policy. The Nazis would have closed down Oskar's operations. His Jewish "business coaches" were indispensable partners in his success.

Oskar had built a network of extraordinarily talented operatives in Płaszów. His successful work as a spy for the Abwehr allowed him to develop an anti-Nazi espionage ring. Ever the cunning spy, he regularly visited the camp when Göth had business in town. In this way, Oskar frequently talked to the likes of Stern and Pemper with the commandant none the wiser. Guards at the camp welcomed his visits because he usually had some gifts to distribute. "Keeping the whole affair afloat required constant 'gifts' at every level of the Nazi bureaucracy,"[63] Emilie Schindler said. "Oskar purchased everything on the black market from diamonds, works of art, wine, caviar, chocolate, to woman's lingerie. Dozens of items that were scarce or impossible to find Oskar was able to procure, and he then showered these rarities on the Nazi decision makers who held the lives of his workers in their hands. When Nazis saw Oskar coming, they could count on the fact that gifts would follow close behind!"[64]

Oskar bribed, lied, manipulated, and deceived. Like many ADHDers, he had honed these skills over many years. Being the object of criticism and scorn, as most ADHDers are in school, becomes hard to bear, and those with quick and creative minds often start inventing cover stories to deflect the negativity. I can say from personal experience that lying quickly becomes addictive. A successful deception leads to a deep and fulfilling high that longs to be repeated. There is something supremely satisfying about defeating a system, or an individual, that one feels criticized or oppressed by. Oskar used this capacity, one that he excelled in, to save people. But without his prior negative experiences, this would not have happened.

Raising Schindler

☐ Mindful that those of us with ADHD, and other learning differences, unconsciously create negativity to make life more intense, stop reacting. If your loved one seems to be baiting you into an argument, you can say, for example, "Oh, you're trying to get me upset. Are you bored? Are you feeling deprived of stimulation?" Your creative responses will go a long toward helping your ADHD loved one understand his or her unconscious behavior. The less you emotionally react, the more we will be challenged to accept responsibility for our own choices, and, yes, our own cerebral hard-wiring.

☐ Many people who have learning differences, like ADHD, have very high levels of empathy. Aware of this, it becomes crucial for you to get your loved one involved in volunteer activities. I have had many people volunteer at animal shelters, homeless shelters, Habitat for Humanity, and Blight Busters, helping tear down blighted building in inner-city neighborhoods. For young people, you can have them form friendships with developmentally challenged folks, do chores and run errands for elderly people in your neighborhood, or participate in litter clean-up activities at local parks and rivers. Find a way to get your loved one involved and exercising his or her muscles of empathy. In helping others, we help ourselves so much more. In the folks I work with, building self-esteem is usually accomplished, at least initially, by finding ways for them to help others.

☐ Time and again, I have found that proper channeling and nurturing of the energies and talents of people with learning differences, especially ADHD, leads to powerful changes in the world. Like Oskar, these folks frequently find the world an oppressive place, and so they are primed and motivated with an almost instinctual desire to change it.

☐ A great deal has been made lately about mindfulness, the idea that we can train ourselves to be more present in the moment and develop the ability to watch ourselves. Oskar Schindler clearly did not have this capacity. The historical record suggests he was, by and large, a prisoner of his mood swings, impulsivity, and fleeting passions. Unlike Oskar, we now have an understanding that mindfulness is something that can be taught, a possibility that gives us the opportunity to put people with ADHD more fully in control of their choices and of their lives. Like any intervention, however, ADHD people have a nagging habit of getting excited and then forgetting to do it. I cover my own journey into mindfulness in Appendix 1. This will offer you some tips and understanding to help your loved one, and maybe even yourself, become more mindful.

NOTES

1 Oskar expressed frequent shock at the upside-down world of Kraków and the Third Reich. He was so shocked that from the very beginnings of his time in the city, he began to warn Jews, like Yitzhak Stern, about Nazis raids and roundups. I crafted this series of dialogues with these realities in mind, as well as from interviews and eyewitness testimony.

2 This dialogue is crafted for flow, but it derives from the sayings of Oskar and the mindset he certainly had toward what was going on around him.

3 To understand how much control Hans Frank exerted, one can look at a word play Germans used. The General Government was also called Frankreich. This word means France, but it also means "Frank's empire," demonstrating that Hans Frank was a virtual dictator. I learned this from David Crowe.

4 "Nuremberg Trial Defendants: Hans Frank," Jewish Virtual Library. Online. Available at https://www.jewishvirtuallibrary.org/jsource/Holocaust/Frank1.html.

5 Heydrich was assassinated by British-trained Czech partisans in spring of 1942. He left behind him, however, many a "true believer" who continued his anti-Semitic fervor.

6 The record teems with examples that prove Oskar's get-rich-quick mindset.

7 "Nuremberg Trial Defendants: Hermann Wilhelm Göring," Jewish Virtual Library. Online. Available at https://www.jewishvirtuallibrary.org/jsource/Holocaust/Goering1.html.

8 Oskar experienced guilt from the very start of his arrival in Kraków. This plagued throughout the war, and it was in fact captured in the movie by Spielberg.

9 "Inside Story of Secret Talk to Generals," *Chicago Tribune*, 18 October 1942. Online. Available at http://archives.chicagotribune.com/1942/10/18/page/9/article/reveals-hitler-called-his-axis-allies-nitwits.

10 Schindler had essentially a once-in-a-lifetime opportunity, and he clearly understood this.

11 Crowe, O'Neil.

12 Joseph Aue was, unbeknownst to Schindler, a Jew. He used his cover to hide in plain sight of the Nazis.

13 Crowe, O'Neil.

14 This quote takes some license, but is corroborated by Crowe and O'Neil in their characterization of Schindler's relationship with Stern.

15 Crowe, O'Neil.

16 This is a reworking of an actual quote. Crowe, O'Neil.

17 This line comes from Spielberg's film.

18 This is a reworking of an actual quote. Crowe, O'Neil.

19 This name is of a real person who was a friend of the Schindlers. But here, this name serves as an amalgam of the numerous people who made this very same sort of statement.

20 Several sources have discussed the relationship between Bankier and Schindler—Pemper, Crowe, O'Neil, E. Schindler—and here I have given a composite name to those remarks for literary flow. I could not find the name of the actual person who said this line, so I invented one. "Janka Olszewska" is my creation.

21 *Schindler's List*. Dir. Steven Spielberg. 1993. Universal Pictures. DVD.

22 While Stern and Oskar did not have much contact before the establishment of the camp at Płaszów, Oskar nevertheless considered Stern's advice absolutely indispensable to his success.

23 These remarks are based on several sources with whom Oskar spoke before and after the war.

24 In interviews with Robin O'Neil, Mietek Pemper was hesitant to divulge too many of Schindler's faults. O'Neil, in fact, pledged that he would not make certain criticisms public. What is part of the historical record, however, is Schindler's extremely impulsive nature, which was also described as impatient.

25 O'Neil, Crowe.

26 O'Neil.

27 O'Neil; this is not a direct quote, but it is accurate in its assertion.

28 Ibid.

29 Ibid.

30 "Nazi Conspiracy and Aggression," (2005). A Teacher's Guide to the Holocaust. Online. Available at http://fcit.usf.edu/holocaust/resource/document/DOCPER9.htm.

31 Shirer, 959.

32 Eichmann, A. (1942). "Minutes of the Wannsee Conference," The Progressive Review. Online. Available at http://prorev.com/wannsee.htm.

33 O'Neil, and Pankiewicz, T. (1987). The Cracow Ghetto Pharmacy (translation by Henry Tilles of Apteka w getcie krakowskim). New York: Holocaust Library, 1987.

34 O'Neil.

35 This quote is based off of O'Neil's research that Oskar tried on multiple occasions to penetrate the security cordon around Belżec. Emilie Schindler confirmed that Oskar never got closer than three miles from the camp.

36 O'Neil.

37 Nowak, L.P. (2004). The History of Chełmno Commemoration, Arkadiusz Kamiński (trans.), Museum of the former Extermination Camp in Chełmno.

38 Ibid.

39 Shirer.

40 Shirer, 946.

41 Shirer, 951.

42 This quote is based on the fact that Heydrich, and true-believing Nazis of his ilk, stated on numerous occasions that Jewish people had no place in the Reich economy. This put him in direct opposition to Oskar's efforts to save his workers by strongly declaring their essential nature to the war effort.

43 This is a direct quote corroborated by numerous sources, including O'Neil, and testimonies of numerous survivors.

44 O'Neil.

45 This exchange between Oskar and Emilie is corroborated using Emilie's remarks about how and why Oskar hatched the plan to move his workers.

46 Ibid.

47 Oskar gave similar accounts to his wife (See Schindler, E.), Schindler Jews, and numerous other witnesses.

48 Pemper, Mietek. (2005). *The Road to Rescue: The Untold Story of Schindler's List*. Hamburg, Germany: Hoffman und Campe Verlag.

49 I have no record of such a conversation taking place, but I am confident this is a subject that Oskar discussed with his inner circle.

50 Ibid.

51 Ibid.

52 Holocaust Research Project. (2014). The Trial of Amon Goeth. Online. Available at http://www.holocaustresearchproject.org/trials/goeth1.html.

53 Ibid.

54 O'Neil, 73.

55 O'Neil, 95.

56 Pemper.

57 Pemper.

58 Pemper and O'Neil.

59 Pemper and O'Neil.

60 Pemper.

61 I paraphrase here, drawing from O'Neil, Pemper, and Crowe.

62 O'Neil.

63 See Schindler, E.

64 The whole operation was built to a large extent on bribery. Schindler made his money on the black market more than he did in legitimate business ventures.

65 I must give credit for this idea to Daniel Amen and his book, *Healing ADD*. Although I do not agree with a lot of what he says in that book, the chapter titled "Games ADD People Play" is inspired and very helpful.

Chapter 5

It's fine to celebrate success
but it is more important to heed the lessons of failure.

—Bill Gates

Amazing Deeds

THE NAZIS EXHIBITED bottomless determination in attempting to exterminate the Jewish people. That determination ultimately came from the top leadership, Hitler and Himmler, and the action came from their subordinates, who considered obedience a sacred and honorable duty. Adolf Eichmann, the SS lieutenant colonel who organized the transports of Jews to death camps, and his friend, Rudolf Höss, commandant of Auschwitz, had several conversations on this topic in 1944, a time when Germans with their brains still intact realized defeat was inevitable. "If we exterminate all the Jews in the east," Eichmann told Höss, "world Jewry can never recover. This is more important than winning military battles. And this is our duty because the Führer has ordained it."[1] Not rising quite to the fanaticism of Eichmann, Höss, nevertheless, agreed they had no choice but to press on: "I have pledged my life to my country and my Führer and just because things have started to look bleak for us I cannot shirk my duty." Eichmann replied, "You are quite correct, Höss. We are but two of the many horses pulling the wagon and we cannot escape, left or right, because of the will of the driver."[2, 3]

These two major figures in the Holocaust considered the word of the wagon's driver, Hitler, as the will of god. When Eichmann was sending thousands upon thousands of Jews every day to Auschwitz in June and July 1944, Höss, recalled from Berlin back to Auschwitz as a troubleshooter, improvised new machinery of murder and cremation to cope with the unprecedented number of inmates at the camp, brilliantly performing his "duty."[4] When no trains were available to transport the Hungarian Jews directly to Auschwitz in late 1944, Eichmann forced tens of thousands of them to march one hundred thirty miles from Budapest to Vienna; from there he had them assigned to labor camps, where many of them died. Höss and Eichmann were efficient murderers and unquestioning followers who never wavered in their commitment to eliminate the Jewish people. As the Red Army started to reach the death and work camps, they and many other leaders in the SS attempted to move able-bodied inmates to other camps and summarily executed most of those unfit for transport. One famous Jew from Hungary, Elie Wiesel, Nobel laureate and author of *Night*, spent eight months in Auschwitz before being moved several times to other camps, ending up in Buchenwald. The majority of the Jews on these forced marches from camp to camp perished. Schindler was up against a system full of perversely talented individuals who were bent on the destruction of the Jews.

Some fanatics actually believed that Hitler had secret weapons that he would unleash at the last minute to secure ultimate victory for the Fatherland. The majority of SS leaders, however, understood that the war was all but lost, and they wanted to not only preserve their remaining Jewish slave labor force, but also to eventually eliminate potential Jewish witnesses to Nazi atrocities. SS leaders fully appreciated they would be held to account at war crimes trials, and for that reason they sought to hide their crimes. In July 1944, for example, captured SS officers and soldiers were imprisoned and eventually put on trial by the Red Army and Polish authorities for crimes committed in Lublin and Majdanek, a death camp in which the barracks and gas chambers were left fully intact for the world to see. In June 1944, BBC radio broadcasts started naming specific SS men from Auschwitz who would be held accountable for their crimes. Nazi attempts to conceal their crimes failed, largely due to the brave actions of Polish and Jewish escapees who alerted humanity to the dark truth.

From the very beginning, the Nazis' plans called for concealment. They located death camps in remote locations and carefully camouflaged the actual death chambers. The grizzly work of removing the corpses was done by Jews, known as the Sonderkommando, most of whom were gassed every few months so that they could not recount the crimes they witnessed. Furthering their efforts to hide their crimes, the Nazis completely dismantled some death camps, including Sobibór, Chelmno, Belżec, and Treblinka. They attempted the same with Auschwitz, but time ran out and they were only able to blow up the crematoria/gas chamber buildings, the ruins of which can still be seen today (a Jewish rebellion had led to the destruction of Crematoria IV in October 1944). For months before the Soviets overran the camp, SS staff members also went about the gargantuan task of burning documents, but they did not destroy all of them.

An examination of Nazi determination at the end of the war serves to highlight Oskar Schindler's genius in saving twelve hundred individuals, people the SS assuredly saw as potential witnesses to their horrific crimes. What began as a cover for spying activities and then an opportunistic get-rich-quick scheme became a humanitarian mission. Not only did Oskar treat Jews in his factory with respect and dignity, but he began to take initiative to help the wider Jewish population. At first, he cared for individual Jewish people whom he considered friends, but as the war wore on, he increasingly acted, when possible, to help all Jewish people suffering at the hands of the Nazis.[5] Evidence shows the power of this transformation as early as the fall of 1942, when Oskar had himself smuggled out of Kraków in the back of a truck; he made his way to Hungary, where he met with the leaders of Jewish relief agencies.[6] The timing of this visit is important, because at that point in 1942, Germany still thought itself in a decent position to defeat the Soviets and win the war. Some have suggested Oskar only saved his workers to cover up his own crimes and cast himself in a good light at his future war crimes trial. No war crimes trials were foreseen at this time; Oskar's conscience and courage simply drove him to do what was right.

During his visit to Budapest, Hungary, Oskar most assuredly informed the Jewish leaders about the horrors being perpetrated in the ghetto and at the death camp, Belżec, which he had learned about firsthand that summer. He took money from these agencies and distributed it to Jewish groups in Kraków. The blatant and skillful conman, however, exhibited scrupulous honesty in distributing every cent of this money to Jewish groups, not keeping one shekel for himself.[7] Oskar made the perilous journey to Budapest many times. "You know what will happen, Oskar, if you are discovered,"[8] Emilie said. "They will put you in one of those horrific places, Dachau, Auschwitz, or Buchenwald." Oskar replied, "They won't catch me, Emilie." Emilie lived in fear. "They will kill you Oskar," she said. "They will catch you and kill you, like the Czechoslovak government almost did. For God's sake, be careful!" Emilie's fears were well founded. Anyone helping Jews was imprisoned or killed. In fact, Auschwitz Camp I held Polish political prisoners, many of whom were imprisoned, tortured, and eventually executed for helping Jews. Oskar's life was in great danger.

Risking detention and death over and over again, Oskar managed to pull Jewish workers and friends off trains bound for death camps. He bribed Nazi officials to have relatives of his Jewish workers transferred to the factory. On multiple occasions, when Amon Göth had capriciously ordered one of his guards to kill a Jewish inmate, Schindler intervened behind Göth's back, usually bribing the guard with alcohol or inviting him out for a night of drinking and debauchery. The six-member Wohlfeiler family, who worked for Oskar, was suspected of falsifying and possessing Polish personal identity cards.[9] Two SS agents arrived at the factory and showed Oskar some incriminating documents. Oskar brought out some of his finest brandy, and several hours later, the two inebriated SS investigators left the factory without the Wohlfeilers.[10] Oskar had saved an entire family.

Whenever he had advance warning of a Nazi "action" in the ghetto, Oskar kept his workers overnight to avoid death and deportation, thereby saving hundreds and hundreds. He also warned them whenever Amon Göth had planned a visit to the factory so they could make sure they looked incredibly busy. Göth would have a worker murdered at the slightest apparent lack of productivity. "Kill first, make inquiries later" seems to have been Göth's motto. While some could say that Oskar's efforts to keep his workers safe from Göth and the SS simply made good business sense, Oskar could have simply behaved like most industrialists: He could have drained and used up his workers and then exchanged them for new ones, following the example of most German war enterprises, like the industrial giant IG Farben. Used-up workers were, incidentally, usually sent to death camps for extermination. Oskar spent massive sums clothing and feeding his workers as well as

Göth on his horse in the Plaszow concentration camp, 1943 or 1944. *United States Holocaust Memorial Museum, courtesy of Leopold Page Photographic Collection*

providing medical care. Oskar repeatedly broke hundreds of Nazi laws in keeping his workers alive.

In spite of his consistent outwitting and bribery of Nazi officials, Heydrich's henchmen, the Gestapo, arrested Oskar three times, with charges ranging from inconsistent and fraudulent accounting practices to "fraternizing with Jews." Oskar's powerful friends bailed him out on all three occasions. You must understand, however, that once a person entered the clutches of the Gestapo, he or she was rarely able to exit. A person of lesser charisma and commitment would have pulled back on his efforts to help the Jews after the first arrest, and certainly after the second, but Oskar only increased his efforts to save Jewish people as the war continued and arrests became more frequent. Those closest to him describe his behavior as reckless and foolhardy, qualities that were indispensable to his ultimate success. Yes, defying the Nazis usually ended in death. The danger to which Oskar exposed himself steadily rose as the war moved to its eventual end.

Multiple witnesses who worked in the Nazi bureaucracy have testified to another of Oskar's improbable feats, in addition to saving his workers: the successful relocation of his factory. In late 1944, with the uncertainty and fear surrounding Germany's impending defeat, panic reigned and brutality knew no bounds, but Oskar was in part successful because he knew how to take advantage of the panic. One slip up, though, and the whole operation would have collapsed. That panic allowed Oskar to do something no one else did; he moved his factory and his Jewish workers along with it! There was very little, if any, financial incentive for Oskar to do this. Coupled with the fact that Oskar ensured his factory produced non-working munitions, the case is clear that he moved his operations for one reason only: to save his Jewish workers.

On their way from Kraków to Oskar's new installation at Brünnlitz, for example, the men, packed into cattle cars, had to stop at the horrific Gross-Rosen camp which, in the words of one of the Schindler Jews, was run by "bellowing psychopaths in uniforms" with skeletal inmates wandering around like "rag-draped scarecrows."[11] Some Schindler workers did not travel on from this stop, as some changes were made to "the list," largely due to the corruption and greed of Marcel Goldberg, who had worked as an administrative manager under Amon Göth at Plaszów. Goldberg not only sold places on the list to the highest bidder, but took steps to eliminate his enemies by taking them off the list. At Gross-Rosen, these unlucky people perished. Gross-Rosen highlights another example of Schindler's persistence. Two of his workers, Henry and Poldek Rosner, well-known Kraków musicians, had their instruments taken from them at this transit camp.[12] Upon learning of this, Schindler called the camp commandant a few days later. "I have to maintain production of key munitions products," Oskar told him. "Music helps me keep them working. It soothes them and keeps them focused as they perform work that will help Germany defeat its enemies. Now, where am I going to find a violin and an accordion at this stage of the war?"[13, 14] Oskar paid some bribes, and the instruments were returned. He acted with fearlessness in challenging and confronting the sociopaths of the SS.

Even more improbable perhaps than moving the factory was Schindlers ability to secure the release of his female workers from Auschwitz. The train with the women, who had traveled separately from the men on the way to Schindler's new facility, had been routed to the notorious factory of death; once there, camp personnel naturally wondered why so many elderly inmates in the Schindler group were being spared the gas chamber, and there was talk of exterminating them straight away. Spielberg's film shows Oskar bribing a camp officer with diamonds, a plausible assertion. No one knows exactly how Schindler obtained their release, but there is some certainty that bribery of the highest magnitude played a role.[15]

The list of Jewish workers to be saved, *Schindler's List*, was itself a masterpiece of manipulation and deception. It contained occupation, inmate number, and age. Older people had their ages reduced ten to fifteen years, while younger individuals had years added on.[16] The very young and the very old were at high risk for being sent to their deaths. As well, great attention was paid to making sure that people on the list had occupations suitable to the war effort.[17] Rabbis were listed as semiskilled metal workers, scholars as engineers, and musicians as metal polishers. The list was scrutinized over and over by Nazi officials, and incredible care was taken to ensure that nothing looked amiss. Wisely, Oskar left the details of the list to the

Jewish laborers at work constructing Schindler's factory at Brunnlitz, 1944.
United States Holocaust Memorial Museum, courtesy of Leopold Page Photographic Collection

Jewish men who worked at the camp offices. Marcel Goldberg wielded incredible power over the list, and his influence is one of the darker aspects of the Schindler saga.

While Oskar seemed to care less and less for his own safety, his efforts to keep his workers safe intensified. When he moved the factory to Brünnlitz, near his home town in Czechoslovakia, he quickly sought to dominate and subdue the SS guards. "My workers," Oskar told SS Commandant Leipold, "will sleep right on the factory floor, where guards will not be permitted. That cuts down time to and from sleeping quarters and raises productivity."[18] The commandant replied, "But Herr Schindler, this is totally against regulations."[19] Appealing to logical and patriotic reason, Oskar overcame this objection: "Regulations are designed to help us win the war. What I am trying to do, Commandant, is help our troops by making more munitions." Leipold dropped the matter, and of course, all the

SS personnel attached to the camp received edible and alcoholic favors which certainly paved the way for Oskar's success in keeping them almost completely separate from his Jewish workers.

In April 1945, Leipold, under orders from his superiors, had plans to liquidate the camp, i.e., murder the Jewish inmates. His subsequent actions show that he was determined in this case to obey orders and had been somewhat ashamed of not having been more stringent with Schindler. Oskar was not directly informed of this plan, but he figured out the truth when he observed SS guards digging large pits in a location away from the factory.[20] On an unseasonably warm spring evening, in one of his most noteworthy, ingenious, and comical moves, Schindler got Commandant Leipold extremely drunk. Leipold, under the effects of intoxication, made a confession to Oskar.[21] "I feel useless, Herr Schindler, sitting here and guarding Jews,"[22] he said. "I should be serving the Fatherland and be up at the Russian front doing my duty. Brave men are dying." Oskar replied, "I will help you, Herr Commandant. Come outside and we will get you battle ready." Oskar then convinced Leipold to continue their drinking session in the warm spring air and showed him some grenades he happened to have on hand.[23] "Come on," Oskar goaded him. "We've got to get you ready for the front." The commandant gave in and the two men engaged in "hand-grenade practice." The explosions caused such a stir in the surrounding area that General Schoener,[24] whose army headquarters were nearby, stopped by the factory in person to investigate. The next day, the general showed up and summarily informed Leipold, "I have seen to it, Commandant, that you are relieved of your duty. You are unstable, unreliable, and certainly undeserving of such a plum posting as this."[25] The next day, Schindler, ever the double agent, was seen in his Horch limousine driving the commandant to the military front.[26] Leipold's replacement was much more placid and easy to influence. Schindler saved his workers once again with extraordinarily inventive manipulation, although many, many Jews were not so lucky. As the end of the war approached, the Nazis went on a killing spree, hoping to annihilate potential witnesses. The day before the Red Army arrived to take over Lublin, Poland, for example, the SS shot seven hundred Jewish and Polish prisoners at the Majdanek death camp. To the benefit of those he helped, however, Schindler was the rare puppet master who knew how to carefully pull Nazi strings.

It was not only *his* workers who benefited from Oskar's manipulative genius; he helped any Jew, or any person, who came into his orbit. In January 1945, a train car was left by the Nazis in the town close to Oskar's factory. Oskar received a phone call from the station master at a nearby train depot. "Herr Schindler,"[27] the station chief spoke. "There is a train here with something close to one hundred Jews on board, and many of them are still alive."[28] Inside the train car, eighty-six freezing inmates, who had been transported from a subcamp of Auschwitz, the brutal cement factory of Goleszów, hovered on the verge of death, having been essentially left to die. Schindler arranged with the local station to have the train taken to his facility. Under protests from the SS, Oskar brought them to his infirmary, and he and Emilie saw to it that these men were nursed back to health. Some of them literally had had their skin frozen to the planks in the train car. Extra rations were brought in, as well as necessary medicines, the latter of which at that point in the war were particularly expensive. Of these eighty-six men, seventy-four survived the war, thanks to Oskar and his wife. In the last month of the war, Oskar saved dozens more, stragglers the SS did not know what to do with, whom he welcomed into his factory. From the time he moved his factory toward end of 1944 until the end of the war, Oskar lived life with a purposefully frenetic pace. He bribed officials from Kraków to Prague and all the way to Berlin to get the necessary permissions to move his factory. He outwitted dozens of Nazi officials and thwarted repeated attempts to murder his workers. That period of time is a case study in the unique successes people with ADHD can enjoy when they have the right stimuli and a deep sense of purpose.

While twelve hundred or so owed their freedom and their very lives to Oskar as the war ended, Schindler himself became a fugitive, temporarily wanted by the Allies as well as by Czechoslovak authorities for his prior treason. He fled the gates of the factory into a life of failure. He engaged in one ill-advised business venture after another, and spent the last thirty years of his life more or less in poverty. Absent extraordinary intensity, intensive support, and the stimulation of living life on the extreme edge, Oskar fell apart.

A Flawed and Failed Genius

Oskar's wanderlust got the better of him after the war, as he flitted between Europe, South America, and Israel. His driving obsession in the three decades after the war revolved around obtaining grants from relief agencies and the German government. With the encouragement of his Jewish workers, now his only real friends, he sought compensation from the German government and relief agencies for having spent his entire fortune to save them. Just as he had been protected by powerful Germans during the war, powerful Jews assisted him after the war. Esteemed Nazi hunter Simon Wiesenthal knew of Schindler and wrote a letter on his behalf:

> As director of the enamelware factory in Kraków and later in Brünnlitz, Schindler saved a great number of Jews. The best that we can do now is to show the gratitude for our protection of 1,200 Jews. In the name of the Jewish Committee of Upper Austria

Schindler in Munich with a group of Jews he rescued, 1946. *United States Holocaust Memorial Museum, courtesy of Leopold Page Photographic Collection*

I ask you to kindly do everything you can to help Director Schindler.[29]

He received money from Jewish relief agencies and eventually from the German government. He also received financial assistance from individual former workers. The state of Israel even invited him to plant a tree in the Garden of Yad Vashem as one of the "righteous among the nations," one of the highest honors the nation can bestow.[30]

Even with a great deal of support, recognition, and admiration, Schindler could not pull things together. He left for Argentina in 1949 with money from relief agencies to acquire a radiator factory, though he never followed through with this plan. He instead did quite a bit of gambling and drinking in

Buenos Aires. His next venture, the scheme involving nutria fur coats, failed because he did not work and left his wife attempt to run the operation, not to mention that neither of them had any experience in this type of business. Frustrated that luck did not seem to be going his way in Argentina, Oskar left the country and Emilie was completely on her own. His next venture, a manufacturing operation, failed because, as he claimed, his German workers were anti-Semitic and out to get him. Without financial and emotional support from his former Jewish workers, Schindler would not have been able to get by.

Mietek Pemper met with him many times, offering him direct assistance in obtaining financial compensation. Pemper talks about how he tried to give Schindler a road map of the steps he needed to take in order to get the money.[31] Schindler's attitude was, "I want the money and I want it now." Getting the money required paperwork, documentation, and obtaining affidavits from witnesses, all details that Oskar lacked the patience to pursue. In spite of his resistance to following procedures, his former workers helped him get some grants and a small pension that allowed him to subsist in his later years.

Rampant mood swings, an inability to delay reward, and ever-increasing consumption of alcohol handicapped Oskar's attempts at happiness. Worries about money plagued him every waking moment. Asked what was bothering him, Oskar would frequently answer, "No money." His problems, however, were of a very complex nature, and Oskar seems to have had little grasp of that reality.

War: What Is It Good For?

Some engines run on diesel, while others on gasoline. Race cars and rockets often run on nitromethane, which burns without needing much oxygen for combustion, and gives more power per stroke. Oskar had one of these latter type of "engines," and the war gave him the fuel that allowed him to soar to great heights. The postwar years did not afford him the fuel he needed, so, like trying to run a rocket on gasoline, the engine of Oskar's brain sputtered. There is no doubt that he had cerebral liabilities: a predisposition for addiction, a low threshold for boredom, an extremely impulsive nature, mood issues, and almost no patience. The war awakened Oskar's brain, giving it the fuel that allowed him to thrive, but after May 1945, it was as if parts of Oskar's brain simply went to sleep.

People with ADHD often have this experience. Sometimes, great fires of brilliance ignite, helping the ADHD individual accomplish extraordinary feats, which are sadly followed by depression, addiction, or simply the malaise of boredom that haunts the ADHD community. Generals George S. Patton and Ulysses S. Grant also shared this trait, both academically underachieving military geniuses who struggled with excessive drinking, mood issues, and malaise when not fully engaged in a grand pursuit. Both men stand, however, as among America's greatest generals because when confronted with the greatest of challenges, they functioned at their absolute best.

As Microsoft founder Bill Gates has counseled, we often learn the most about ourselves by examining our failures. From that perspective, Schindler's life shows that those who fail most miserably can also achieve greatness. Oskar's life shows that it is of primary importance to understand our weaknesses as well as appreciating the necessary circumstances for us to optimally function. For both those who have ADHD and those who do not, Oskar's life demonstrates the magic that can happen when we find the necessary support to examine our strengths and weaknesses and put together a program of success uniquely suited to our authentic way of being. The war offered Oskar a rare situation that he never was able to recreate, but with the right amount of insight into himself, I am convinced he could have gone on to perform great services to humanity.

Addiction: Negative Intensity

More than anyone I have come across in my research, Schindler survivor Rena Ferber Finder succinctly captures the essence of Oskar's nature and his wartime transformation: "I think he was a gambler and loved to outwit the SS. In the beginning it was a game. It was fun at first. He joined the [Nazi Party] to make money. But he had no stomach for the killing. He enjoyed the wheeling and dealing and doing outrageous things— living on the edge. But then he realized if he didn't save us, nobody would."[32]

Like generals Grant and Patton, Schindler thrived in extremely intense situations. When life was more mundane, however, he turned to alcohol to self-medicate during periods of boredom, malaise, and depression. In fact, alcohol created a negative kind of intensity, which for a person like Oskar is preferable to no intensity at all. Oskar's drinking actually slowed down quite a bit during the war, during which he operated with great and purposeful intensity. However, it picked up again afterwards, exacerbated by a worsening gambling habit. Oskar's increasingly addictive behavior was perhaps an unconscious attempt to reinvigorate his brain. After the war, he never escaped the cycle of addiction, a fact that significantly contributed to the postwar tragedy of his life.

People with a brain like Oskar's have an atypical way of experiencing reward, rooted to some extent in the pleasure centers of the prefrontal cortex. The human brain is basically set up for the experience of reward, a sense of satisfaction and pleasure that leads to the motivation to repeat certain experiences. If a certain action leads to a feeling of satisfaction and pleasure, the brain responds by giving us impulses to repeat it. Over time, a normal brain will be able to delay gratification, keeping motivation high even though potential reward could be somewhat far off. Oskar's brain caused him extreme difficulty in delaying reward. ADHD people, like Oskar, will usually take a relatively small but immediate reward over a much larger but longer-term one. Said another way, ADHDers, like Oskar, do not generally stay motivated without ongoing high-levels of external stimulation.

People with brains like Oskar's are at a significantly elevated risk for addiction. Having this atypical way of experiencing reward coupled with low self-esteem and lack of success in school make for a potentially dangerous mix. To function optimally, all human beings require an experience of satisfaction and pleasure. When these needs are not met, the human mind swings into action to try to find ways to make up for this deficit. When people abuse substances, like alcohol or cocaine, and feel a semblance of the pleasure and satisfaction that usually eludes them, they can easily become hooked, a fact made worse by the physical dependency that can arise. The "high" that is experienced from use of the substance also has the effect of temporarily masking unpleasant emotions. From this perspective, substance abuse is an escape from reality, arising from ineffective coping. Incidentally, many of the same gene variants found in people with ADHD are often found in addicted individuals, a fact that not only points to the genetic basis of both conditions, but also highlights the fact that both arise not out of poor character, but from cerebral predispositions.

People like Oskar, those with ADHD, crave intensity and only seem to thrive when they have it. I, for example, suffer from severe anxiety along with my ADHD. But when I am on tour, speaking in multiple countries in a short period of time, my anxiety and most of my ADHD symptoms simply disappear, without medication. Taking a plane or a train to a new city or country every other day fills me with a sense of purpose and energizes me. Seeing new sites, meeting new people, and pushing forward into a new day of travel give me a sense of adventure, a feeling of being in the flow. At home, I often feel trapped, ensconced in a malaise that does not easily give up its hold, but even just the possibility of adventure can energize me. In the weeks before a trip, I function with superhuman focus and energy. The trick for me is to always make sure I have an adventure on the horizon. Otherwise, I can succumb to my addiction, online video games.

When a person is wired with a need for intensity, if he or she does not get that need met positively, he or she will invariably find ways to meet it negatively. Science continues to show that some people simply have genetic variations that make their brains seek out novelty and excitement. These are individuals with a built-in need for new challenges and adventures. Holding back the need for intensity progressively increases the strength of the impulse and drive to have it. Trying to hold back the need for excitement is tantamount to a person trying to live life against his or her inner nature. My personal and professional experiences, as well as the life of Oskar Schindler, show that the longer the need goes unmet, the more destructive its eventual expression will be. "Boredom slows Oskar down and sends him temporarily into despair,"[33] Emilie said, "but that despair will always lead to Oskar doing something stupid. The despair leads to drunkenness, gambling, philandering, and incredibly short-sighted and ill-advised business decisions. Since the war, he just cannot stay on track." People with ADHD who are untreated and undiagnosed will almost never be able to "stay on track."

Oskar knew he was unsatisfied with his life, and he had a strong sense that something was forever missing. The reasons for his predicament seem to have eluded him. The concept of Attention Deficit Hyperactivity Disorder was in its infancy, as were Alcoholics Anonymous and medical understandings of mental health. He did not receive any mental health diagnosis, and even if he had, the medications and treatments were not very effective at that point in time. Those close to Oskar often assumed that his troubles were the result of character flaws and a lack of willpower. Emilie chalked up a great deal of his missteps and failures to immaturity, frequently referring to Oskar as childish, not willing to fully grow up. Others simply blamed his troubles on his heavy drinking. Oskar most often blamed anyone and everyone, not accepting much in the way of personal responsibility. While we can use science to shine the light of understanding on Oskar's behavior, ultimately there were things Oskar could have done to change his situation. If he had looked at his choices and set out to change the unproductive and destructive ones—and if he had received appropriate mental health treatment—the second half of his life would have turned out quite differently.

Beyond the Blame Game

Almost every human being experiences obstacles and some level of adversity. Most highly successful people, in fact, frequently recount rampant failures as their greatest teachers, as Bill Gates has often pointed out. During World War II, Oskar failed often but he never stayed down, always picking himself back up and finding a new perspective, an innovative approach. In August 1944, for example, he persisted all the way to the head office of the Reich Arms Inspectorate in Berlin, after local officials in Poland did not give him permission to move his factory and workers. Passed around from department to department, Oskar would not take no for an answer. He had enough wealth to easily retire to Switzerland and live like a king for the rest of his life.[34] Instead, he used vast sums of money to bribe corrupt officials of the Third Reich and to call in favors to those who owed him. He also used his deceptive and resourceful nature to make many in the Arms Inspectorate think he was the relative of one of the heads of the department, Lieutenant General Maximillian Schindler. This incorrect assumption made many bureaucrats much more complaint with his wishes. Oskar did not blame anyone; he rose to challenge after challenge by using his gifts to the fullest extent and doing the seemingly impossible: relocating his factory and his workers.

Something in him broke after the war. Those persistent, driven behaviors seemed to cease; Oskar became a chronic complainer and tried to cast himself as an unfortunate and innocent victim, in order, perhaps, to come up with some sort of explanation for his consistent failures. A letter in 1955 to his friend Yitzhak Stern shows just how far, psychologically, the hero had fallen:

> [My] farm has produced great debts, which I could balance out during normal times. But agriculture is first of all a business of the good Lord, dependent on numerous factors, and second, there is only one harvest per year, which means that I have very low capital flow. Necessary investments with extremely high interest rates were not successful. At least my wife enjoys animals, which makes the work a little more fun for her. Due to the enormously high social and food costs I gave up breeding poultry three years ago and have focused solely on the breeding of nutria. But even with nutria the relation between costs and sale prices is getting worse every year. Three months ago I began preliminary plans to sell half the farm as construction land to ease my debts. But the plans of the revolutionary government [in Argentina] to devalue the peso will delay this sale of property and the construction of apartments on it for several months. Right now, everything seems paralyzed.[35]

Conversations Oskar had with many of his friends at this time suggest he knew he was not pursuing the sort of ventures he was suited for, but he still blamed his circumstances and did not move into full acceptance of his role in creating failure. In this letter to Stern, he does not admit to his lack of hard work and his absorption by heavy drinking and gambling. He blames financial circumstances, bad luck, and the Argentine government. This same pattern continued, and in 1963, as his cement business was failing, he wrote again to his former workers, Stern and Bejski, and rustled up even more excuses:

> Unfortunately, we are experiencing a winter in Germany that I have not seen in many, many years. It even created problems for stable construction firms. I am very pessimistic about the upcoming weeks.... Friendly talks at conference tables do not produce wages and without wages the workers are not motivated to work. The fact that I am physically and psychologically near the end is caused not only because of my coronary heart problems ... but also the ever tiring fight against hidden attacks.[36]

Again, no personal ownership is taken, as Oskar blames the workers, the weather, and some hidden conspiracy against him. The once mighty defender of his Jewish workers indulged in the blame game, the least effective response to overcome adversity. Circumstances may present legitimate difficulty, but individual response is the only thing each of us ultimately controls.

People who deal with ADHD individuals will often experience this blame game. "I am not doing well in school because of the teacher," ADHD children will often say. "Mrs. Johnson just doesn't like me." From early on, many ADHDers take to blaming others, which is understandable because failure is hard for a child to take. I have found, personally and professionally, however, that the extent to which we succeed is directly proportional to our level of personal responsibility and accountability. I can only change how I respond. I may need support, but if I ask for it, that becomes the first step to responding to adversity in a healthy and productive manner. For example, as a writer who has ADHD, I experience serious bouts of writer's block. When this happens, I have a choice: I can either let myself stay blocked or take steps that will help dissolve the block. Now, sometimes my tricks to inject myself with motivation do not work. At that point, I have another choice: suffer in silence or call in the cavalry—my close friends and colleagues. The choice is to go it alone or get support from others.

Ultimately, I have to be willing to take full responsibility. When I do that, I generally find success. I am a master of excuses and blame, an aptitude honed over a lifetime with ADHD and a troubled upbringing. I have found that blaming makes me temporarily feel better. Many with ADHD, myself included, have a reservoir of inadequacy that is activated by mistakes and failure. This inadequacy is so painful and persistent that we often automatically react by blaming other people and situations supposedly beyond our control. I have found that by allowing the inadequacy to come up—instead of always pushing it down—it loses its power, and our energies can more quickly move to finding steps to take to right a wrong or turn failure into success. Not taking responsibility for one's actions is almost always rooted in this deep sense of inadequacy, of a feeling of being irreparably flawed. Taking responsibility not only involves owning choices, but also the internal reactions that underlie them. Oskar, like all people with ADHD, needed to work on delving into himself and coming to terms with the full truth. Self-inquiry and honesty would have helped him end the blame game and empowered him to get enough support to consistently make life-affirming decisions.

Support, Support, Support

During the war, Oskar not only had intensive support to make life-affirming decisions for himself, but also for hundreds and hundreds of others. Asking for and getting support is in many ways the opposite of the blame game. When we ask for support, we exhibit the ability to acknowledge that we cannot do it alone, along with freely admitting our own weaknesses. When the blame game holds sway, by contrast, we steadfastly deny our weaknesses, and thus eliminate the possibility of compensating for them.

Asking for support is a powerful aptitude that successful people almost always possess. In reaching out to others, I honestly acknowledge my weaknesses and my strengths. Oskar exhibited this capacity during the war. His support team had depth. He had at his disposal some of the leading business-men of pre-war Kraków, accountants, business owners, and high-level deal makers among them. He went to Kraków to continue spying for the Abwehr, but also to start a business and get rich. Before he settled on which business to buy, he sought out many experts, including Yitzhak Stern and Abraham Bankier, two highly-respected and well-known business leaders in the city. To his credit, Oskar recognized their wisdom and took their advice to purchase the Rekord company, which he renamed Deutsche Emailenwaren Fabrik. He had the opportunity to pick from many Jewish businesses in receivership but persisted in performing due diligence to find the one that best fit his needs and capabilities. Oskar understood he was out of his element in this endeavor, and circumstances conspired to put him in touch with the right people. These men, seeing his genius and decency, continued advising and empowering him throughout the war.

After the war, Oskar seems to have kept mostly his own counsel on which businesses to get involved in, a fact that had consistently disastrous results. What I strain to understand is why Oskar did not get Stern, Bankier, and Pemper more involved in his business plans. Oskar seems to have fallen back into a self-sabotaging tendency. Unfortunately, many ADHDers possess, along with an instinctually rebellious nature, a strong urge to go it alone. We are so prone to snatching defeat from the jaws of victory. Acknowledging and overcoming this liability is crucial for success.

Mission

Finding support gets a whole lot easier when we are surrounded by people who have the same sense of mission. Motivation and persistence are generally only possible for ADHD people when we are hot on the trail of a powerful and purposeful goal. Like Oskar, people with ADHD struggle so significantly with details that holding a job and doing it well often prove elusive. We do not need a job; we need a mission.

One of my ADHD coaching clients, Jim, a man in his mid-fifties, has worked as a carpenter for forty-eight different companies, and has also struggled with substance abuse. Each time he gets a new job, he beams with enthusiasm and talks about how wonderful it is, and how he wishes he had found this company years before. Two to three weeks into the job, he typically starts complaining, and altercations with co-workers can ensue. "When I was drinking, I would not start bingeing until I started to become bored and frustrated with my job," he said. "I needed to work, so I used alcohol to at least have something else to look forward to. All day long at work, I would think about drinking once I got off."

I have worked with Jim on owning his own choices and finding ways of sustaining motivation and making the job more intense. Like Oskar, Jim has behaved as if the next dream job lay around the next corner. The potential of new possibilities keeps him going, but sustaining the present work situation proves impossible because Jim does not have a purpose; his jobs have felt like nothing more than a necessary evil.

A development last year has changed his outlook. I hooked him up with a friend of mine who owns a large construction company that also does extensive community outreach. Jim started volunteering with this firm every Saturday, while still working his other job. Essentially, he helps children learn skills and build self-esteem. He started going to inner-city areas and leading teams of teenagers in fixing up blighted neighborhoods. He not only saw the visible results of his efforts, beautified neighborhoods, but also understood that he was changing the lives of young people. My friend's firm was so impressed with Jim that they hired him full-time and he now works one day a week, paid, spearheading the neighborhood outreach project. But Jim still volunteers with the teenagers almost every Saturday. So far, this newfound purpose has ignited a focus that has allowed this man to become a reliable and consistent employee. "I think that this is what was missing," he recently told me. "I just would get a few weeks into a job and feel like there was no point. Working with these kids makes me feel like I am actually fully living life. Their lives are real, sometimes sad, and being around them makes me feel like my life is real, too, two divorces and seven alcoholism relapses later."

Oskar would have completely resonated with Jim's story. Making cement, tending to chickens and nutria, and overseeing the minutiae of a business felt like a depressing grind to Oskar. While he claimed that he wanted a new business so he could make money, he lacked the self-understanding, as well as the professional help, that would have made him aware that making money was not sufficient to consistently arouse his brain. Yes, he impulsively pursued the fineries of life, but the promise of the luxury items that money could buy did not create sustainable motivation in Oskar. He languished in boredom and depression in business after business, yet when people's lives depended on him, he hid in a truck all the way to Budapest, riding two hundred fifty miles on dusty, pot-hole-strewn roads. When Jewish lives hung in the balance, he braved a cordon of SS security to see what was really going on at the Belżec death camp, risking his life. At the end of the war, he traveled feverishly back and forth to Berlin and to the offices of SS decision makers in Poland. Yes, Oskar was a man on a mission, but more than that, he was a man like almost all ADHD people I know who needed a mission to function. Just like his brain required intensity, Oskar needed to help people; he needed to know that his actions had deep purpose. Among ADHD people, this is simply normal.

This is the reason I believe that ADHD people represent a population uniquely suited to changing the world. Perhaps part of the reason is that we have the experience of feeling marginalized, left out of the mainstream. We often feel oppressed by school and other systems that do not recognize our uniqueness. We have an ingrained experience of suffering that makes many of us deeply empathetic to the plight of others. As Dr. Moshe Bejski, Schindler survivor and Israeli supreme court justice, said, "Oskar cared not only for us as a group, but he also made each of us feel as if we were cared for individually."[37] While he lacked follow through and persistence, Oskar had an incredibly high level of emotional intelligence, effortlessly connecting to the pain and plight of others.

He did not, unfortunately, have enough self-reflection to realize why the war brought out his genius and why his success evaporated thereafter. So, he tried to go back to "business" as usual. He should not have tried to raise animals for fur or run a company that made cement. There was nothing intrinsically engaging for him in these and all his other ventures. They were all simply a means of making money, and they were devoid of any deeper purpose for Oskar. He should have worked for the Red Cross helping refugees, or for the World

Health Organization protecting people in developing countries against epidemic disease. He would have thrived if had found a situation where he could have helped the oppressed, or at least assuaged people's pain.

For anyone who wants to empower a person with ADHD, please know that you do the most when you help us help others, because that is exactly what we are uniquely positioned to do. So often, we find ourselves maligned and marginalized, but when we genuinely help others, we find a way to more fully enter the community of human beings from which we often feel far removed. This experience provides the motivation that we usually lack.

Helping alleviate the pain and suffering of others fuels our brains. Just like we have trouble filtering extraneous stimuli, like noises in a classroom, we are not good at filtering out the pain that we see in others. Many of us with ADHD have a unique ability—that can sometimes feel like a curse—of viscerally experiencing the pain of others as if it were really our own. Having ADHD also means that it is difficult, perhaps impossible, to turn off this empathic power, so the only way I know to deal with it is to find ways of decreasing the pain and suffering in the world. Help a person with ADHD find a mission and you will change not only that individual's life, but quite possibly the whole world. As it says in the Talmud, "He who saves one life saves the world entire."

The intensity of the war, intensive support from his wife and workers, and a sense of mission combined to break the spell of failure and depression in the life of Oskar Schindler. He gave people hope, one of the most precious commodities in the hell of Nazi-controlled Europe, and he saved lives. But external circumstances robbed Oskar of the ingredients for success. Lacking self-reflection and increasingly finding himself stunted by addictive behaviors and substances, Oskar spiraled to rock bottom and never really got up again.

Raising Schindler

If you have a child or loved one who exhibits some or perhaps many of the traits of Oskar Schindler—whether or not he or she has been diagnosed with ADHD—you will certainly have experienced a great deal of frustration, both in understanding your loved one and in dealing with the school system. You have probably known in your innermost being that he or she has incredible strengths and potential. Hopefully, this book has confirmed your suspicions, and helped give you renewed hope and a new, more productive mindset.

You have assuredly witnessed time and again your loved one not performing up to his or her potential. You now know that school is particularly tough because that institution measures people on a narrow band of aptitudes and not only ignores strengths, but pathologizes them. The very things that make your loved one unique—high energy, spontaneity, natural out-of-the-box thinking, intense creativity and imagination, and an ability to change focus quickly—will be experienced by many teachers as annoying at best, if not as outright affronts to authority. Thus, the school system not only appraises your loved one's value by almost exclusively evaluating skills he or she struggles with—sitting still, memorizing and regurgitating information, and keeping silent—but also denigrates the very aptitudes in which the individual excels. Self-esteem suffers, often leading to a lifelong inner voice of self-doubt, a voice that unconsciously sabotages future relationships, jobs, and overall chances for a happy life.

While Oskar received physical punishment, in addition to the powerful disapproval of his teachers, your loved one likely receives a steady, but subtle, diet of mental abuse. Abuse may seem like a strong word, but I have no reservations, because I consider it abusive when a system consistently fails to help a person, especially a child, reach his or her potential and instead denigrates his or her very being. The result is that our society ends up having a huge segment of the population with loads of potential who nevertheless doubt themselves and their chances for making a positive impact on this world. In a recent incident in the United States, an eight-year-old boy with ADHD was handcuffed by a police officer, a fact that demonstrates the continued lack of understanding that ADHD young people experience. So, what can we do?

First of all, as parents we must become tireless advocates for our children. Yes, teachers have a hard job, one that is becoming increasingly difficult. But we cannot be too concerned with their plight. Our first and primary goal must be to protect our children. They spend all day in an environment in which the majority of people in positions of power are not effectively trained. This environment puts our children in the charge of someone who has no idea of their neurobiological uniqueness, no clue of their potential strengths. In this age of financial cutbacks in education, we may have to be the ones who educate teachers and administrators alike. We have to insist that our children are valued and receive appropriate accommodations. We may not be able to do this alone, so I strongly encourage parents to get help. There are advocacy groups all over the world. Find one and get in touch with a group of parents for mutual support. Together, we can create a world where, instead of seeing a child with Oskar's predispositions as a misfit or a problem, we say, "Hey, this child could be another Schindler." We then try to find as many ways as possible to nurture his or her innate strengths and preserve and enhance self-esteem. With adults, we must encourage them to forge a ring of support, get treatment, and find ways to counteract the massive amount of negative messages they have internalized. We need to NOT FOLLOW Oskar's example and instead find treatment for the negative aspects of the condition.

Even before our children go to school, we must pay close attention to what they naturally love to do. Perhaps your child has an unusually high energy level. Perhaps he or she has an instinctual interest in tools. It could be that even as young as two or three years of age, a propensity for sports or certain physical activities becomes apparent. Perhaps your child appears to live in his or her own world, and thus likely is highly reflective and imaginative. Once we pay close attention and develop a reliable sense of our child's innate skills and preferences, we then must get to work to find activities that nurture them. We must make this same effort with adults, encouraging them in their talents and gifts and helping them find ways to express their uniqueness.

If you see some of Oskar Schindler in a loved one, it is highly likely that he or she will be what we call a hands-on learner. This is an individual who may not find a great deal of motivation for memorizing or listening to the presentation of information, but his or her intelligence and interests will become activated when there exists a distinct purpose. Also, when information regurgitation and memorization are required, this type of person will do best when in motion. So, if you have to help your child with spelling words, have him or her take a walk with you, get on an exercise bike, jump on a trampoline, or run up and down the stairs between words (Safety first!). If you have an adult ADHDer who is studying for a certification exam in his or her field, you can do simple methods, like recording information and having him or her listen to it while on a walk. Movement can be integrated into study; you just have to get creative. You can also consult my previous book, *Movers, Dreamers and Risk-Takers: Unlocking the Power of ADHD*. It is a book largely geared toward helping people, especially parents, spouses, and teachers, create a positive and pragmatic mindset with their ADHD loved ones, offering detailed strategies and suggestions to develop their innate learning and perceptual preferences. The bottom line is that there are incredibly effective ways of working with people of Schindler's disposition. If we take great care in nurturing them, I am of the firm belief that we will be creating the change makers our world so desperately needs.

In spite of your best efforts with younger folks, school may continue to emit destructive messages. You must work hard to nurture activities and interest that allow your child to feel good about his or her abilities. Telling your child, "You're really smart," pales in effectiveness with finding and encouraging an activity or interest that engenders a deep, inner feeling of competence.

Take a page from Oskar's playbook and find ways your child or loved one can help others. Is there a child in your neighborhood with some developmental challenges who could use a friend? Does your church need volunteers to help do clean up? Is there an elderly person in your area who needs yard work done, or someone to talk to? Find service opportunities for your child and praise him or her profusely for doing them. Rather than just telling your child you are proud of him or her, talk on the phone to a friend or relative, communicating to that person how proud you are, making sure your child is within earshot. Your child has received an overwhelming number of negative messages; you now need to work at counteracting them. Remember, with the right support and stimulus, the Oskars in our midst change this world for the better.

Oskar Schindler's life sends the undeniable message that individuals who learn differently can and do change the world. If you or a loved one has a lot in common with him, I ask you to look deep inside and to be open to help from the outside. Have the courage to inquire within yourself and totally admit both your strengths and your weaknesses. You cannot do it alone, so start the process of finding support. First, look in your own family, talk to close friends, and then search the wider world. Find a support organizations near you; the Internet makes this exceedingly easy. If you or your loved one struggle with addiction or depression, get those conditions treated. Carefully study Oskar's life and you will see that if he can do it, so can you, but in order to succeed with consistency, your loved one needs to get treatment and support! And please, do not try to use this book as a substitute for professional help. ADHD people are designed to shake up this world and make it a better place for everyone. Let the shaking begin!

NOTES

1 This conversation between Eichmann and Höss is one woven from the memoirs of both men. Höss, R. (1959). *Commandant of Auschwitz*. London, U.K.: Orion House. "Eichmann's own memoirs describe Nazi death machine," (2000). CBC News. Online. Available at http://www.cbc.ca/news/world/eichmann-memoirs-describe-nazi-death-machine-1.198014.

2 This line has been quoted many times, and comes directly from "Eichmann's own memoirs describe Nazi death machine," (2000). CBC News. Online. Available at http://www.cbc.ca/news/world/eichmann-memoirs-describe-nazi-death-machine-1.198014.

3 Incidentally, much evidence has shown that by the last year in the war Hitler was suffering from Parkinson's disease, which degrades movement and slows mental agility. In addition, Hitler's doctor was giving him strong drugs, one of which was essentially crystal meth. This is the driver the two men were obeying.

4 Throughout their writings, both men repeatedly talk about the importance of doing their duty. Eichmann, however, seems to have had zeal and enthusiasm to a much greater extent than Höss.

5 Wundheiler, L. (1986). Oskar Schindler's moral development during the Holocaust. *Humboldt Journal of Social Relations*, 13 (1 and 2).

6 O'Neil.

7 Ibid.

8 As with most issues in their relationship, Oskar throws caution to the wind, while Emilie expresses worry. Many such exchanges certainly took place.

9 O'Neil.

10 Ibid.

11 Brecher, E. (1994). *Schindler Survivor Stories*. New York: Plume, p. 1.

12 Pemper, O'Neil.

13 Oskar was quick on his feet when confronted about his workers. No one knows exactly what he said to get those instruments, but bribery was most certainly involved. This example highlights a tendency by Schindler of justifying his moves as good business sense, as decisions designed to increase productivity and help the war effort.

14 The Nazis, incidentally, frequently used music at the work camps and death camps, hoping to keep the prisoners calm. Some Jewish inmates at camps like Auschwitz and Treblinka were actually full-time musicians whose job was to play as the inmates lined up and unwittingly walked to their deaths. During "selections"—processes that determined which inmates would stay in a camp and which would be sent to their deaths—music was often used to keep movement in time and inmates in step. For these reasons, when Oskar suggested that music was important to keep work humming along, there was actually precedent for this line of thinking.

15 Schindler scholar David Crowe points out that they may have simply been released because the SS. followed orders and paid close attention to paperwork.

16 Pemper.

17 Ibid.

18 Leipold tried to do the "right" thing and follow Nazi protocols, but he was no match for Schindler, who cowed him into submission with trickery, bribery, and threats.

19 We do not know his exact words, but the record is clear that Leipold protested many of Schindler's factory policies.

20 O'Neil.

21 O'Neil.

22 I got this story from O'Neil, and there are various versions of it from different sources. O'Neil took great pains to corroborate this account from multiple sources.

23 Ibid.

24 I do not know the general's actual name, so I invented one.

25 We do not have the general's exact words, but we do know he was upset with the commandant's behavior and saw to it, after his visit, that Leipold was dismissed.

26 Ibid.

27 I relied on Crowe, Pemper and O'Neil for this one.

28 This story comes from O'Neil, Pemper, and Crowe.

29 O'Neil, 185.

30 Oskar, as most ADHDers, had his detractors. One of the former owners of the factory that Oskar purchased made charges of brutality and theft. The full truth is difficult to ascertain, but regardless of what dirty deals Oskar may have done, the factory was in receivership because it was a Jewish-owned business. Oskar did, however, engage in some brutal behavior and ruthlessness in the early years of his business, in efforts to fully secure his ventures.

31 Pemper discusses these issues in his own book, and in interviews with Robin O'Neil.

32 Brecher, 23.

33 Emilie talked extensively about the impact of boredom on Oskar, and these lines are somewhat my creation from things she said in her own memoir.

34 O'Neil.

35 Crowe, 501-502.

36 Crowe, 510.

37 Crowe, 530.

My Holocaust Heroes

It is no accident that I chose to write a book that deals with the Holocaust. The Holocaust has intrigued me since I was a boy. I have come to believe that human nature has an undeniable dark and twisted side, a fact that the Holocaust makes clear, and that challenges each of us to look deep within. As Gandhi said, "The only devils in this world are the ones running around in our own hearts. That is where all our battles should be fought." I subscribe to a Jungian view of evil, that we all have a dark side, a part of ourselves we would prefer to ignore. I believe the extent to which we admit to the deep propensity we each have for selfishness, hatred, and evil is the extent to which we will be able to prevent these destructive forces in our society.

Some brave people go beyond self-examination and find a force more powerful than evil, a willingness to lay down their lives for others. This rare attribute transcends the human impulse of self-preservation and rises to perhaps one of the most spiritually-evolved states human beings are capable of. I was educated by nuns, the Sisters of Loretto, who highlighted this scriptural verse: "Greater love has no one than this: to lay down one's life for one's friends" (John 15:13).

Maximillian Kolbe

I was raised Catholic and grew up in a town so thoroughly homogenous that I did not even know what a Jew was until high school. For some reason, the Holocaust interested me from a very young age. I watched the BBC's World at War when I was ten years old and can still remember the emotional disturbance I experienced when I watched the episode on the Holocaust. One survivor who was interviewed talked about how little food they had in the Warsaw Ghetto and how his brother constantly screamed, "bread, bread, bread." This man detailed the brutality of life in the ghetto and listed the multiple relatives he had lost at the hands of the Nazis. That very first exposure to the Holocaust, and that man's face, have stuck with me.

Shortly after my thirteenth birthday, I, like all Catholics of that age, was called to make my Confirmation, a sacrament which represents one's becoming sealed in the faith. As part of that ritual, the young person picks a saint who will serve as something of a spiritual guide, a model of the Christ-like life. My teacher was very strict about this aspect of the process of Confirmation, and gave us detailed instructions that we were to pick a saint to whom we felt personally connected. It was October, and I still was not able to find a saint to whom I felt that connection, and the next day was the deadline. After Church that day, for some reason, I picked up the Church bulletin to read that just a few days before, Pope John Paul II had canonized a man named Maximillian Kolbe, who gave his life so that another man could live. There was quite a large article on him, and I read the whole thing several times.

Kolbe had been imprisoned in Auschwitz because he had published anti-Nazi newsletters through his Franciscan Monastery Press. He and several of his fellow priests had also used their monastery to hide refugees wanted by the Gestapo as well as Jews. He continued to act as a priest while in Auschwitz, drawing the ire of his Nazi jailers, and he was subjected to beatings and constant harassment. Not long into his incarceration, three inmates from the camp escaped. Consistent with Nazi custom, ten inmates were chosen to die, part of a system of reprisals the Nazis hoped would deter future escape attempts. The deputy camp commander, under Rudolf Höss' orders, picked ten men to be starved to death in an underground cell of the infamous punishment building, Block 11. One of those unfortunate men, Franciszek Gajowniczek, screamed in agony, "My wife! My children!" Hearing this, Kolbe volunteered to take his place.

According to an eyewitness who worked in Block 11, Kolbe led the other nine men in prayer and helped keep them calm and peaceful. Kolbe was the last one alive, living almost two weeks in a darkened death chamber with no food or water. Every time the Nazis checked on him, he was kneeling in the center of the cell, apparently deep in prayer. Impatient, they injected him with carbolic acid to finish him off. Kolbe defied the Nazis through his sacrifice and his ability to ignore the suffering of the moment and connect with a higher power. In that factory of suffering, Auschwitz, Kolbe sanctified human life by willingly accepting death and facing it with dignity.

Just like Schindler, Maximillian Kolbe was not without his flaws. Evidence exists that he published a few articles before the war that were critical of the role of Jews in Poland's economy. Regardless of some scant critical views of Jews, however, he hid and helped hide over two thousand of them from the Nazis. Maximillian Kolbe, like Oskar Schindler, was not perfect. The two men show the potential in the human heart for redemption, to make mistakes and then somehow have the courage to care more about others than about oneself to the point of risking one's life or even willingly sacrificing it.

Tadeusz Pankiewicz

As the horrors unfolded in Kraków, one brave Polish man witnessed it all. When the Germans established the ghetto in 1941, there were four pharmacies owned by non-Jews located within its boundaries. Three of the pharmacy owners accepted the German offer to move their businesses into the Aryan area of the city, far away from the misery of the ghetto. One of the owners, however, decided to stay, a decision that confounded the Nazis. This man, Tadeusz Pankiewicz, witnessed and recorded all of the barbarism that took place in Kraków: the roundups, daily beatings, murders, deportations to death camps, and finally the complete liquidation of the ghetto. Pankiewicz's pharmacy represented, along with Schindler's factory, one of the Kraków Ghetto's few safe havens and a hub of underground activity. Some have described the pharmacy as a "clearing house" for information regarding escape routes out of the ghetto. Many Jews in that city only survived the Holocaust because of Pankiewicz's efforts.

In his memoir of these experiences, The Kraków Ghetto Pharmacy, Pankiewicz details numerous, and corroborated, instances of helping Jews escape the ghetto, risking his own life to save others. He provided disguises, hair dye (blond hair made it easier for Jews to pass as Aryans), and assisted dozens of Jews in obtaining false papers. Some Jews were able to hide in his pharmacy on numerous occasions, and thus avoided being gassed to death in Belżec and Auschwitz. More than once, Pankiewicz came within a few minutes of being deported himself, as anyone in the ghetto during rounds-ups who was not in a German uniform was at risk. When the Germans sealed the ghetto prior to deportations, orders were issued that no non-Jews were allowed in or out. In one instance, Pankiewicz was arrested by an S.S. soldier while walking through the ghetto and was rushed toward the deportation area. The fact that he showed the document granting him permission to be in the ghetto did not cause the soldier to reconsider. Only at the last minute did a high-ranking S.S. officer intercede on Pankiewicz's behalf, pulling him out of the deportation line.

Events in the ghetto regularly put his life in danger, as stray bullets and chaotic violent actions came threateningly close to the pharmacy. Pankiewicz determined to be the beacon of hope to those in the ghetto. In 1983, Yad Vashem bestowed upon him its highest award, Righteous Among the Nations, for his heroism and bravery.

Dr. Albert Battel

Many of us fail to appreciate that quite a few Germans opposed the Nazis and regularly engaged in small, and large, acts of resistance. Ordinary Germans defied the Nazis, and many of these people were put into concentration camps, while others were simply executed. Albert Battel was a lawyer who, like many Germans, was in the army reserve. Shortly after the campaign in Russia began to get bogged down, he was called up to active service.

Oberleutnant Albert Battel was fifty-one years old in 1942, and was called up to assist in supervising armaments production at a time when Germany was experiencing a severe manpower shortage, both of workers in its factories and soldiers in the field. The army stationed Battel in Przemysl, a town not far from Lublin, in the far eastern part of Poland. Like Schindler, Battel was suspected of being a "Jew lover" and had even been called out by the Gestapo. Before the war, for example, he loaned money to a Jewish friend of his, and during his tenure in Poland was witnessed shaking hands with some of his Jewish workers.

The S.S. scheduled the first large "resettlement" action against the Jews of Przemysl for late July, 1942. On July 26, Oberleutnant Battel, with the support of his superiors, sent in troops to block the bridge over the River San, the only access point to the ghetto. S.S. soldiers, who had been charged with rounding up the Jews of Przemysl, tried to make their way over the bridge. The sergeant in charge threatened, under direct orders from Battel, to open fire if they persisted. Battel led a caravan of trucks to the ghetto gates later that day and when the S.S. guards—who had previously sealed off the ghetto—refused him entry, he threatened to call his headquarters and send for reinforcements. He rescued over one hundred Jews from certain death. These Jews were placed under the protection of the Wehrmacht and were thus protected from deportation to the Belżec extermination camp. The remaining ghetto inmates were sent in the days that followed to their death at Belżec. Of the twenty-two thousand Jews in Przemysl, fewer than three hundred are thought to have survived.

Reports of this incident came across the Kraków desk of Oskar's drinking buddy, Julian Scherner, and from there, went up the chain of command all the way to Heinrich Himmler. Battel's actions were described as outrageous, reprehensible, and criminal. Himmler took an active interest in the investigation into Battel, even sending memos about the incident to Martin Bormann, Hitler's chief of staff. Himmler vowed to arrest and prosecute Battel after the war for crimes against the Nazi state. Battel died in obscurity, but thanks to the efforts of Dr. Zeev Goshen, an Israeli researcher and lawyer, Yad Vashem named Dr. Albert Battel as a Righteous Among the Nations on January 22, 1981.

Appendix 2

Jewish Resistance

People often express confusion about the seeming lack of Jewish resistance to the Nazis, but this mindset can be traced quite simply to a lack of information. Many of us are only familiar with the Holocaust because of a documentary we watched on *PBS*, A&E, or the *History Channel*, or perhaps from a two-paragraph section in our high school history textbook. The image that most of us come away with from our scant exposure is of Jews being naïvely and passively led to slaughter. One aspect we generally fail to appreciate is that the Nazi move toward genocide came in systematic and gradual stages, and no one could appreciate or foresee that Nazi moves to progressively exclude Jews from society would lead to industrial murder. The Nazis understood the value of giving the impression that in spite of present suffering, there was hope. *Resettlement* trains, the Nazis maintained, would transport Jews to a better life, to a place where they would find work, away from the horrors of ghetto life. The Nazis, some of history's most masterful manipulators, used the human tendency to hope as a tool of supreme deception.

First, they progressively deprived the Jews in Germany of their civil rights. Laws were passed forbidding Jews from practicing certain professions and from using public spaces, like parks. Marriage to non-Jews was prohibited, Jewish professors and teachers were fired, and Jewish doctors were not allowed to treat *Aryan* patients. All the while, Josef Goebbels, Minister of Propaganda, cranked out anti-Semitic films, articles, and radio programs, steadily bombarding the German public with lies that many actually came to believe. Millions of Germans gave credence, for example, to the preposterous notion that the Jews had sabotaged Germany's chances of winning World War I. While some latched on to such lies, those Germans who saw through them were hard-pressed to resist, as they knew that speaking out against the Nazis, as well as helping the Jews, could lead to incarceration in a concentration camp. Thus, Hitler could go further without fear of any significant protest or resistance, so the Nazis confiscated Jewish property, and finally, after years of brutal treatment, deported Germany's Jews to the east. Jewish people were, unfortunately, historically accustomed to such mistreatment and many reasoned that Hitler and his followers were just another hate-filled anti-Semitic storm that, although severe, they could weather just like they had done many times in the past.

People of this mindset ended up being terribly, and tragically, wrong. Hitler and Himmler not only terrorized and deported the Jews of Germany, but they learned from their experiences and made the whole process utterly systematic. The terror Germany's Jews suffered was exported to conquered lands, albeit it in an unbelievably more horrific manner. While the process of dehumanization and deportation in Germany happened over almost a decade, it proceeded with rapacious speed in conquered territories. Killing squads, called the Einsatzgruppen, followed the German Army into Soviet lands and rounded up Jews, marched them outside of town, and shot them in the back of the head. The bodies then dropped into pits that had been dug beforehand. The Germans were aided in these horrors by auxiliary troops from the conquered lands, as well as allied countries. Well over one million Jews were killed in this manner, along with seven-hundred thousand other victims. Those people had of course heard of Hitler's treatment of Jews in Germany but none of them suspected the wholesale slaughter the Nazis unleashed.

The majority of Jews, prior to being murdered, were crowded into ghettoes, where many starved to death or died from one of the many epidemic diseases that plagued these densely-packed misery zones. In these closed living areas, the Nazis could fully enact their campaign of brutality and murder against the Jews away from prying eyes, away from the potential disapproval of the German public and the rest of the civilized world. They even tried to give the impression that they were treating the Jews humanely. They created a *model camp*, Therezienstadt, to showcase the *productive* lives Jewish people were living. Inspectors from the Red Cross visited on several occasions, reporting that the Jews received adequate nourishment, had productive employment, and even enjoyed some leisure activities. Of course it was a sham, but the massive effort undertaken gives evidence to the lengths the Nazis went to hide their crimes from the world and to deceive the Jewish people. Throughout Europe, Nazi efforts to exterminate the Jews involved extreme and carefully-planned deception.

When Jews were deported in the summer of 1944 to Poland from Hungary, some groups were kept in Auschwitz family camps for a short while. They were then instructed to write to their families—a common Nazi practice called the Postcard Deception—to tell them about how good life was in their new surroundings. Shortly after these letters were written, most of these unfortunate Hungarian Jews were sent to the gas chamber. Their family members still in Hungary had *reliable information* that good things awaited them, and were thus less inclined to put up a fight. Two Hungarian Jews forced to write postcards did, incidentally, fight back. Josef and Samuel Stern signed their cards *Josef Revim* and *Samuel Blimalbiscj. Revim* is Hebrew for "hungry" and *Blimalbiscj* Hebrew for "without clothing."[16] The postcard lie was used in many countries all across Europe. In some ghettoes, Jews who willingly signed up for deportation were promised extra rations, sometimes jam, butter, and bread, which were virtual luxuries at that time for people who were starving. The Nazis made every effort to give the Jews hope that deportation, *resettlement*, would lead to a better life.

The death and work camps were not only camouflaged from the outside world, but the S.S. took great pains to make sure that the Jews entering these extermination facilities had little idea of what awaited them. The death camp at Treblinka was made to look like a legitimate train station, with train schedules displayed, flower boxes, and even an orchestra playing, a practice used in many Nazi camps. Jews arriving to a death camp would sometimes hear an S.S. man say, "Hurry up! The soup is getting cold." The Nazis needed the process to go quickly. First of all, the less time people languished on the railway platform, the less likely they were to get wind of what awaited them. Secondly, on many days they were killing so many thousands of people they just did not have much time. In Auschwitz, legitimate-looking public health posters were posted in the undressing room just outside of the gas chambers. These *health announcements* warned of the dangers of typhus and the consequent *importance* of disinfecting and delousing showers, which people were told they were to undergo. This trick was taken further at Treblinka, where an S.S. guard, during the first months of the camp's operation, demanded one zloty as a *fee* for showering; he collected this *fee* in a booth outside of the entrance to the gas chamber in another attempt to maintain the deception until the last possible moment. The clothing hooks in the undressing rooms in Auschwitz had numbers, and the victims were told it was very important they remember their number to retrieve their clothes after the *shower*. Mammoth efforts were taken to conceal the truth from their victims until the very last moment.

Extreme brutality, of course, also played a role, as the roundups in the ghettoes generally involved random shootings and constant beatings. Jews were whipped, clubbed, and smashed in the head as they were herded into cattle cars for a train journey that could last for days. Deprived of food, water, and sanitary facilities, many individuals on these train treks died in route. When the doors were finally slung open, the unfortunate occupants were thoroughly exhausted, most of them hyper-focused on simply finding a few sips of water. "Hurry up," S.S. men would bark. "The quicker you move, the quicker you'll get food and water." These people were in no shape to struggle, lacking all sustenance and having just spent countless hours huddled together in a train car with piles of excrement and dead bodies. Non-compliance meant a truncheon to the head, or a rifle butt to the back. The beatings and extreme deprivations they endured meant that few had any energy to resist. Yet, Jews did resist, a fact which few of us ever discover.

From mid-July 1942 to mid-September 1942, the S.S. managed to send over a quarter millions Jews from the Warsaw ghetto to their deaths in Treblinka. The remaining inhabitants came to understand that the destination of the trains leaving the *Umschlagplatz*, the point of departure, was not deportation, but death. Around 60,000 Jews continued to work and reside in the ghetto, and many of those determined they would fight the Nazis. In January, the Nazis tried to round up more Jews, but ghetto fighters fought back and S.S. squads succeeded in only taking five thousand, far short of their *quota*. Deportations were halted thereafter until April 1943, when the official Warsaw Ghetto Uprising commenced. With only scant weapons, these brave fighters battled not for freedom, but for the dignity of the Jewish people, knowing full well they would likely die. Tasked with destroying this revolt, General

Jürgen Stroop did not succeed militarily. Resistance was too stiff and the Jewish fighters had far too many subterranean bunkers to which they could flee. Eventually, in early May, Stroop essentially decided to obliterate the entire ghetto, using flame throwers, explosives, and incendiary devices to destroy each and every building, bunker and hiding spot. He flooded many deep underground bunkers and used poisonous gas to flush out the last defenders. Well over ten thousand Jews were killed in the uprising—many burned to death—and the fifty thousand or so captured were sent to concentration and death camps. The brave band of Jewish fighters had held the German Army at bay for well over a month.

The Jews of the Sonderkommando in Auschwitz, on the other hand, were only able to keep German soldiers at bay for a day, but this was enough time to do something extraordinary. The Sonderkommando, or special unit, was the unfortunate work detail that did the *dirty work* of the crematoria/gas chamber complex. They helped the victims undress, assisted in getting them to quietly go into the gas chamber, and then pulled out and disposed of the dead bodies, an obviously grizzly set of tasks. They also shaved the corpses, went through each and every mouth to remove gold teeth, and sorted the victims' possessions. The Sonderkommando, who were kept isolated from the rest of the prisoners in the camp, received a temporary reprieve from death in the gas chamber and also benefited from extra rations. Wishing to cover up their crimes, the S.S. at the camp regularly murdered the men in the Sonderkommando as part of the ongoing attempt to silence potential witnesses to their crimes. In the summer of 1944, over four hundred thousand Hungarian Jews were sent to Auschwitz, most of whom died. But as summer turned to fall, the gas chambers slowed down, and the men of the Sonderkommando realized their turn was coming since their *services* were no longer in high demand. Such a suspicion was confirmed in mid-September when S.S.

officers informed two hundred of the Sonderkommando they were being transferred to another camp. They sent them first to Auschwitz Camp I, and, using their well-honed skill of deception, gassed these people in a building that had been previously used for disinfecting clothes so that these men did not suspect their fate.

Underground resistance groups in Auschwitz quickly hatched plans to burn down the barracks in the camp and blow up all the crematoria. Several women in the camp conspired to steal, conceal, and deliver gunpowder to members of the resistance movement. Ester Wajcblum and her fourteen-year-old sister Hana worked in the munitions factory along with Regina Safirsztain and Ala Gartner. These four women smuggled out gunpowder that was supposed to go into German artillery shells. Roza Robota worked in the clothes depot, and was able to help get the explosives to the adjoining men's camp. Various methods were used for this smuggling operation including hiding the gunpowder in dead bodies that were taken to the Sonderkommando for disposal.

On the morning of October 7, 1944, news spread through the camp that three hundred members of the Sonderkommando from Crematoria IV and V were going to be transported away. Realizing that they were going to be murdered, the remaining members of the Sonderkommando leapt into action. They attacked the S.S. guards who came in later that day to take them away and they then set fire to Crematoria IV. Seeing this, the Sonderkommando at Crematoria II tried to escape but were captured and/or killed. In Crematoria I, a particularly nasty and violent S.S. guard was thrown alive into an oven. In all, four hundred and fifty one members of the Sonderkommando lost their lives, and Crematoria IV was damaged beyond repair. The four women who made the whole revolt possible were given up by some of the men who were interrogated through torture. When the S.S. interrogated these women, however, they only gave the names of men in the Sonderkommando who were already dead. They showed incredible courage in spite of barbaric torture inflicted for days at a time. They were among the last people publicly hanged in Auschwitz in early January 1945.

A year before the Sonderkommando uprising, on October 24, 1943, a transport arrived at Auschwitz from the Bergen-Belsen Concentration Camp. Following their protocol, the S.S. divided the group into those who would live and those who would die. The latter group was then split again by gender. The men, as was the custom, were led to Crematoria III, while the women went to Crematoria II. The men were murdered without incident, but things did not go smoothly with the women. One extraordinary, but nameless, woman, strongly suspected what was about to occur. She refused to be led quietly into the gas chamber and rallied the group. Neither the Sonderkommando nor the S.S. guards present could calm this woman down. As they moved forward to subdue her, she took action. She threw an article of clothing over the head of one of the S.S. guards, Josef Schillinger, lunged at him, wrestled away his pistol, and fatally wounded him.[17] She shot another S.S. man, Wilhelm Emmerich, who lived, but was crippled for life. Many other women joined with this brave soul, but reinforcements were called in and the rebellion was put down. The next day, Höss ordered reprisals, and thirteen inmates were shot.

Numerous brave individuals actually escaped from Auschwitz, an extraordinarily difficult proposition that mostly ended with not only the death of the escapee but of other prisoners whom the S.S. murdered in reprisal. Auschwitz not only had numerous rings of barbed wire, guard towers, and a full complement of attack dogs, but the camp itself had an "interest zone," an area of 40 square kilometers from which the Nazis had removed Polish inhabitants in order to create a secured area that would minimize potential witnesses as well as make escape more difficult. Many of the houses formerly inhabited by Poles were given to *Volksdeutsche*, ethnic Germans who were fiercely loyal to the Nazis, and who would, of course, report any suspicious activity. This zone also had secondary towers, checkpoints, and posts that the camp guards would occupy whenever an escape was suspected. To maximize chances for success, inmates would prepare a hiding place, and actually remain within the camp or the interest zone for several days, until the camp security alert status was lowered.

One Slovakian-born inmate, Rudolf Vrba, had arrived in Auschwitz in June 1942. He worked for a good amount of his time in the camp's sorting area, called *Canada* by the inmates, which helped him get extra rations and stay alive and healthy. Through the help of his friend, Alfred Wetzler, a fellow Slovakian Jew, Vrba started working as a registrar, a position which allowed him to move easily around Auschwitz. With an almost photographic memory, Vrba kept diligent track of the number of transports that arrived at the camp, their country or region of origin, as well as the approximate number of victims arriving. In the spring of 1944, everyone at Auschwitz realized that obvious preparations were underway to increase the pace of murder. At this time, Eichmann was making arrangements to start sending Hungarian Jews to Auschwitz. Up to that point, political developments in Hungary had kept the Jews safe, but that all changed. Vrba and Wetzler, veterans of the camp, decided that someone needed to tell the world. The two men, with help from other prisoners, prepared a hiding place, a hollow area inside a pile of lumber that lay between the inner and outer perimeter of the camp. At the appointed time, other prisoners screened their activity as they lowered themselves into the inner chamber they had created in the wood pile. Around this area and on their bodies they sprinkled tobacco that had been soaked in gasoline so that the dogs would not pick up their scent. At roll call that evening, their absence was discovered and throngs of S.S. guards swung into action, occupying posts and guard towers through the camp and its "interest zone," in an effort to prevent the prisoners from getting too far. Vrba and Wetzler heard guards and dogs regularly pass within steps of their location, but maintained calm. One S.S. man even climbed up on top of the wood pile, sitting within inches of the two men. They had actually tied felt strips around their mouths to prevent coughing, which could have alerted guards to their location.

After three days, the search was called off, adhering to camp protocol, and the men made the perilous trek from southern Poland into Slovakia. They walked eighty five miles, mostly at night. Keeping off the roads, they still encountered S.S. patrols and checkpoints, and took a few chances by asking for help from some Polish farmers along the way. Without the assistance of Poles, they may not have made it. Not only did Polish farmers provide them with safe places to sleep and food, but one Pole helped them find a safe spot to cross the border into Slovakia.

After fifteen exhausting days, they crossed the Slovakian border and made contact with members of the Jewish Council, who they then alerted to the horrors at Auschwitz. The men of the council did not initially believe what they heard. To test the veracity of the claims, they brought out documents that detailed all the Slovakian Jews who had been deported to Auschwitz. Vrba's extraordinary memory won over the council as he effortlessly recited hundreds of names of Slovakian Jews he had either worked with in Auschwitz or who he knew had been murdered. Under the council's urging, Vrba and Wetzler then crafted a document, which later came to be known as the Vrba-Wetzler Report, that contained detailed diagrams and maps the two men drew. They wrote about the use of slave labor, confiscation of property, S.S. managerial methods, and the mass murder of Jews. Their report was given to the pa-

pal nuncio in Slovakia, and from there, traveled to the Vatican and then all over the world, read by government officials at the highest levels. Some scholars credit the Vrba-Wechsler Report with motivating Admiral Horthy, the pro-Nazi leader of Hungary, to eventually stop the deportations, thereby saving over a hundred thousand Hungarian Jews. From this perspective, Vrba and Wetzler represent the largest successful effort of Jews saving other Jews during the Holocaust.

Like these two brave men, thousands upon thousands of Jews attempted escape all across the Nazi empire, but most were caught and killed. In Sobibór, a death camp in the far east of Poland, on the other hand, the largest and most successful escape took place. Jewish inmates of Sobibór, along with Soviet prisoners of war, rose up on October 14, 1943. That day was chosen because Commandant Reichsleitner and Sergeant Wagner, the most brutal member of the camp's S.S. contingent, were both away on leave. Those who planned and executed this operation took full advantage, like Oskar Schindler, of S.S. strengths: punctuality and predictability.

The workshops in Sobibór processed confiscated Jewish property. The S.S. basked in the booty that came through the camp, and many would regularly instruct the prisoners to be on the lookout for certain articles, from a leather coat or boots, to a certain type of gold watch. On that day in October, Jews from the workshops had made appointments with many S.S. guards and officers, who showed up on time to try on, they thought, a coat, a new pair of boots, or view a newly-acquired precious item. As these men entered the workshops precisely at their appointed times—which had been carefully staggered ten to fifteen minutes apart—they were summarily killed with axes and daggers. They had hoped to kill all the S.S., decapitating the command of the camp, thus leaving the Ukrainian auxiliary guards in disarray. The Ukrainians and the S.S. figured out what was happening, but not until eleven S.S. men had been executed. Before the prisoners could follow through on their plan to simply walk out *en masse* through the front gate, they came under a hail of machine gun fire. They ran toward the fences, cut through the barbed wire, and made their way through mine fields to the woods, the whole time under intense gunfire. Of the six hundred prisoners in the camp, three hundred escaped, but a good many of them were hunted down and killed. Only fifty prisoners survived the war, which was many more, however, than would have lived if their fate had been left in the hands of the Nazis.

Inmates of death camps like Sobibór knew their likely ultimate fate, which pushed them to resist. A similar mindset took hold in Slovakia in the summer of 1944 as an uprising broke out among numerous segments of the population. Hoping to oust the pro-Nazi government, two thousand Jews participated in this revolt. When the Germans sent in thousands of troops to finally put down the uprising in October, the remaining Jewish rebels fled to the mountains and many joined up with the partisan fighters of Tito in Yugoslavia. Jews fought as partisans all over Europe. The most notable band of Jewish partisans battled the Nazis from the forest. The Bielski brothers came from a large Jewish family in an area called Byelorussia. As the German Army moved into the towns around their farm during the deep advance into the Soviet Union, this family witnessed the full scope of Nazi atrocities. After the Germans killed their parents, some of their siblings, along with many friends, neighbors and relatives, the Bielski brothers—Tuvia, Asael, and Zus—formed a partisan group, initially killing those who had collaborated with the Nazis. The group also cooperated with other partisan groups in harassing Nazi supply lines, disrupting communications, and even blowing up railroad tracks. Tuvia, the leader of the group, saw his mission as not just resisting the Germans, but in saving the lives of Jews. He took in any Jew who needed shelter, and word quickly spread through surrounding areas. Young, old, and sick people found their way to the Bielskis. Like Schindler's factory, the arboreal refuge of the Bielskis offered a rare zone of protection within the madness of Nazi Europe. Jews in the Bielski group married, observed the Sabbath, and worked hard to support the fighters. They made clothes, weapons, and ammunition. They cultivated crops, gathered food, and became proficient hunters. A tight-knit community coalesced around the Bielskis and they could retain their Jewish identities without fear of violence, deportation, or death. Over twelve-hundred Jewish people eventually found their way to the Bielski group and survived the war.

Tuvia and his band of fighters, which perhaps comprised no more than a third of the group at any one time, were a large and uncomfortable blemish to the brutal efficiency on which the S.S. prided itself. Desperate to put an end to Bielski operations, in 1943 they offered a bounty of one-hundred thousand marks on Tuvia's head, a sum that today would be in the millions. Not only did the Bielski group snatch away Jewish victims from the jaws of the S.S., but they also blew up police stations and killed many informants and collaborators the Nazis counted on. Bedeviled by the tenacity of the Bielskis and their partner partisan groups, the Germans martialed twenty thousand troops in the summer of 1943 to track down partisans in the area of Byelorussia the Bielskis operated in. Some group members lost their lives in the battles that followed, but the Bielskis moved the whole group every few days to avoid a pitched battle, and eventually they went so deep into the vast tracts of forest that they defied Nazi attempts to capture them. The Holocaust experiences of the Bielski group are memorialized in a movie, one I highly recommend, which is aptly named, *Defiance*.

Amidst the deception, dehumanization, lies, brutality, and murder on an industrial scale, many Jews found the strength and courage to resist. Some brave souls resisted simply by refusing to allow the Nazis to break their spirits. Others escaped, armed themselves, and fomented open rebellion. The Nazis failed both in their attempt to hide their crimes from humanity and in their effort to destroy the dignity of the Jewish people. Their greatest defeat can perhaps be seen today in broad terms with the success of the diversity movement which seeks to foster acceptance and active valuing of people of different races, creeds, abilities, sexual orientations, and gender. We now see, contrary to Nazi propaganda, that difference and diversity are our inherent strengths in sociological, psychological and genetic terms.

ENDNOTES

1 Braham, R. (2002). *The Nazi's last Victims: The Holocaust in Hungary*. Detroit, MI: Wayne State University Press.

2 Lanzmann, C. (1985). *Shoah*. New Yorker Films.

3 The historical record is replete of examples of this sort of trickery, designed to maintain the illusion of *normalcy* until the last possible moment so that the victims would enter the death chambers as easily as possible. This anecdote comes from Dov Kulka.

4 Lanzmann, C.

5 Piper, F. (2009). "The Mass Extermination of Jews in the Gas Chambers." *Auschwitz: Nazi Death Camp*: Auschwitz-Birkenau State Museum and Douglas Savage.

6 Jarosz, B. (2009). "Organizations of the Camp Resistance." *Auschwitz: Nazi Death Camp*: Auschwitz-Birkenau State Museum and Douglas Savage.

7 "The Revolt at Auschwitz-Birkenau," Jewish Virtual Library, 2016.

8 Ibid.

9 Ibid.

10 Jarosz, B. (2009). "Organizations of the Camp Resistance." *Auschwitz: Nazi Death Camp*: Auschwitz-Birkenau State Museum and Douglas Savage.

11 Swiebocki, H. (2009). "Prisoner resistance." *Auschwitz: Nazi Death Camp*: Auschwitz-Birkenau State Museum and Douglas Savage.

12 There are at least five versions of this story, some of which declare that the woman was well-known Polish dancer, Franceska Mann. All sources agree that a beautiful woman killed Schillinger.

13 Langbein, H. (1994). "The Auschwitz Underground." *Anatomy of the Auschwitz Death Camp* (Edited by Gutman, Y., and Berenbaum, M.), Indiana University Press.

14 The Nazis drafted guard from many of their conquered lands, and Ukrainians filled the ranks in numerous death and work camps in the Nazi empire

15 Yad Vashem.

About the author

Kevin Roberts is the author of *Movers, Dreamers, and Risk-Takers*, and *Cyber Junkie: Escape the Gaming and Internet Trap*. He has appeared on numerous television and radio interviews, recently on ABC and the BBC, and is an acknowledged international expert on ADHD and excessive screen issues. Roberts speaks around the world, delivering his message of hope and empowerment to doctors, teachers, nurses, therapists, parents and young people. He speaks six languages. You can catch him online: www.kevinjroberts.net (Don't forget the "j" in the middle!).